TAKE
THE
STAIRS

TAKE THE STAIRS

Leadership Lessons Learned
from a Lifetime of Service with
Auto-Owners Insurance Company

By Roger Looyenga, CPCU, CLU

With Joe Tye

ISBN: 978-1-887511-24-7

The Self-Empowerment Pledge™ and The Pickle Pledge™ are
trademarks of Values Coach—Paradox 21 Inc.

All proceeds from the sale of this book will be donated to the
Richard and Lorayne Otto Scholarship Fund.

STAIRWAY TO SUCCESS

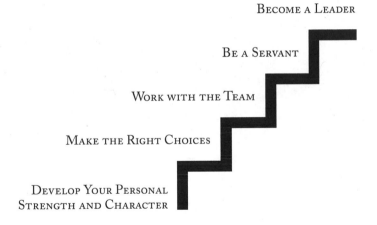

BECOME A LEADER

BE A SERVANT

WORK WITH THE TEAM

MAKE THE RIGHT CHOICES

DEVELOP YOUR PERSONAL
STRENGTH AND CHARACTER

Dedication

To Ann my wife, who is my love forever.
To our sons Justin and Nathan, who are the
pride of their parents.
And to the associates of Auto-Owners—this book
is my gift to you.

Acknowledgments

We are who we are because of the love, concern and care of so many along our journey—family, friends, teachers, preachers, and coworkers; if I acknowledged all of them, I would have my second book. So at the risk of leaving out many people, I especially wish to mention:

My mother and father, for teaching me the core values of life, which are also the core values of Auto-Owners.

Ken Osborne, for your friendship during my youth.

My mother- and father-in-law, Lou and Max Tanner, for inviting me into their family.

Fred (Fritz) Leman, for teaching me important lessons in leadership, and Bob Warner for teaching me the importance of developing relationships with agents (long before the importance of relationship-building became a hot topic in the business world).

Don Jones, Bob Farrell, Bill Perkins, Chuck Ferguson, Peter Legge, George Nordhaus, Roger Sitkins and Emily Heuling—with admiration for all that you have shared with the associates of Auto-Owners, and appreciation for your ongoing friendship.

Herm Arends, my predecessor as Chairman and CEO, who was my mentor and guide as I transitioned into new roles with the company.

Pat VanWormer, Administrator of Executive Services. Thank you for keeping me on the right track with all the details required of the CEO position.

Brad Mitchell, thank you for your spiritual guidance.

Joe Tye—without you, *Take the Stairs* would still be a dream.

The independent insurance agents and their staffs, who help us serve and protect our policyholders. Our shared loyalty makes us a formidable team in a very competitive world.

The senior leadership group, who are a team in the truest sense of that word. I appreciate the support and the friendship you have given me during my 37 years (and counting) with Auto-Owners.

And finally, to Auto-Owners associates. I am continually inspired by your dedication and your passion. It is a privilege to be associated with such an outstanding group of people.

CONTENTS

The First Step: Developing Your Personal Strengths and Character

The Second Step: Making the Right Choices

The Third Step: Working with the Team

The Fourth Step: Being a Servant and
Making a Contribution

The Fifth Step: Becoming a Leader

Foreword

I have been privileged to review Roger Looyenga's new book *Take the Stairs*. My immediate reaction was to make a list of ten people I wanted to share it with. Were I not retired from the agency business, this book would become a key part of my agency team-building meetings, and I would give every associate a copy to read, re-read, discuss in team meetings and, most of all, to influence and expand their own lives and careers.

When I ran my agency, I was focused on the growth and development of my associates to their fullest potential. I still believe that is the foundation of any successful business, which is one reason I created *The Better Way* program as a guide for building a more successful insurance agency. But in today's fast-moving and hypercompetitive world, you also need inspired and empowering leadership. *Take the Stairs* is a wonderful prescription for providing that sort of leadership. And not only in your business, but also in your family and in your community.

This book is not just an academic collection of untried theories. Auto-Owners has been living the values of honesty, loyalty, hard work and the other qualities Roger describes for over 90 years. In the process, they've built one of America's premier insurance companies—one that I've been proud to be associated with for the best part of my own career.

I have worked as a consultant with a number of different insurance companies, and they could all learn important lessons from Roger's book. The people of Auto-Owners reflect the character and values that should be the core foundation of our industry as a whole. For that matter, our entire free enterprise system could stand a healthy exposure to *Take the Stairs*.

Don Jones
Author, *The Better Way*

Introduction

One of my goals in life has been to write a book. A book is something that can live on forever, long after the author has departed. This book is about the choices we have in our lives. These choices all build upon one another, the way each step on a staircase leads to the next higher step. The book consists of short chapters in which I will share with you some of my core beliefs about leadership, and about the choices we all must face, and the steps that we must take, in our work and in our lives. My wife, Ann, suggested the title *Take the Stairs,* and I decided to go with it, because that title happens to be a great metaphor for one of my own guiding principles when it comes to making choices: if you consistently choose the path that requires hard work over the path of the easy way out, you will be much more successful in your career and ultimately much happier in your life.

Take the Stairs has been written for the associates of Auto-Owners. This company has given me so much, I wish to return something in the form of a book. My hope is that you will become a better person as a result of my experiences. In turn, the company will become an even better organization. For a company is nothing more than a group of people working together for the purpose of serving the customer.

Before we get started, let me share with you a little bit about me. I was born in 1946 in Bismarck, North Dakota and grew up across the river in Mandan, the oldest of five children. I was a pretty normal kid. I played basketball in junior high school, but was not good enough to make the high school team; I wrestled in high school, but was not good enough for college wrestling. I also played tennis in high school and played one year on the college team. My major achievement during high school was playing the coronet and later the trumpet. I was lucky to play first chair from junior high to graduation (there were other players, in case you're wondering).

During high school, I was an average academic performer and an above-average performer on the social scene. I had a lot of great friends and liked to have fun with them (but nothing that would get us thrown in jail). Our main entertainment during the weekend was going to a football or basketball game and then "cruising main street" along with all the other kids. Back then gas was only twenty cents a gallon.

Auto-Owners first three core values were exemplified in the years during which I was growing up. HONESTY: crime was almost non-existent. We never locked our house except when we went on a vacation. Car keys were always left in the ignition without worry of the car being stolen. HARD WORK: I worked my last two years in junior high school and four years in high school in a dry cleaning shop. I knew that my family was not able to pay for my college education, and that it would be up to me. That's where PRUDENCE comes in—I worked to save money for my college education.

I went to college in Minot, North Dakota, which is 120 miles north of my home. Minot is famous for being home to a large U.S. Air Force base, and roadside booster billboards as you enter the town with the slogan: "Why Not Minot?" I will always remember the day someone from the Air Force base took out a full-page ad in the *Minot Daily News* summarizing all the reasons for "Why Not Minot?" The first one he listed was this: "The Reason is Freezin'."

I attended Minot State College, which today is a university. The school was small, approximately 2,000 students, which fit my small-town upbringing. Being close to the Canadian boarder, the winters were brutal. I'm talking about wind chill factors of 90 or 100 degrees below zero. During these cold days, I was able to take a tunnel underground to most of my classes. No coat needed, just jeans and a shirt.

There are things in our lives we will never forget. I will always remember my first day of arrival in Minot. I met a new kid in the dormitory and struck up a conversation. He said he'd been the valedictorian of his high school class. I was impressed—until I quizzed him on the number of students he graduated with. His answer—three.

During my stay at Minot State College, I continued my social activities, but became a little more serious about my studies. After all, it was my money funding those tuition checks. I graduated with a major in business science and a minor in psychology. I also participated in intramural football and wrestling, was elected to the student council, and became very active in my fraternity. Being elected fraternity president was my second real lesson in leadership (later I will tell you about my first leadership experience). Serving as fraternity president taught me the value of teamwork. When I took the position, we had $50.00 in our bank account. Because we were the poorest fraternity on campus, we had numerous money-raising projects. We did everything from raking lawns, washing cars and erecting a barbed wire fence around several acres on a farm. Not only did we earn money as a team, we became close to each other, almost like brothers. I see our teamwork at Auto-Owners creating the same collegial environment.

After college, I moved to Minneapolis, Minnesota to embark on a career. Back in 1969, jobs were plentiful. I went through a placement agency and after two days had two job offers. One was with a food company and the other with an insurance company (not Auto-Owners). I took the insurance company job because they paid $500 more a year and they had a nicer company car.

My first job was as a payroll auditor. My territory was Minnesota, North Dakota, South Dakota and Wisconsin. I was on the road 4-5 nights every week. Being single, it was a great adventure. After a year with this company, they wanted to transfer me to Chicago. My choice was Chicago or no job; I chose the no job option and started looking for another. My last day with that company was on a Friday, and I started with Auto-Owners on the following Monday. It was one of the best decisions I have made in my life.

After a year in Minneapolis as a payroll auditor, I was asked to move into Lansing Branch Underwriting. I accepted the offer to move for a career advancement opportunity. Going into underwriting gave me an opportunity to learn the insurance business. I accepted, without knowing a single person in Lansing. Over time, though, the people who worked at Auto-Owners became family, and life was good. One of the people working part time at the company was an attractive young woman named Ann Tanner. The ladies in the office thought it would be "neat" to have Ann spend half a day teaching me data entry as a keypunch operator. That was in 1971. We were married on June 9, 1972 and will be celebrating our 35th anniversary in 2007.

Several months prior to getting married, I was asked by Brice Smith, Assistant Vice President, Agency, to be a Special Agent (back then we called marketing reps Special Agents—not to be confused with Secret Agents!), which would require leaving Lansing. I told him that I would accept on one condition—that Ann would accept my proposal of marriage. That evening I asked her to marry me. She said yes, but she also wanted me to ask her father for her hand. Her father happened to be H. Max Tanner, who was then Auto-Owners First Vice President. It was not as easy, for two reasons. First, I was scared to death and second, he tried to talk me out of it. Either I was really good at selling myself, or I was more stubborn than he was, and he finally gave in.

We were married on a Friday, went up to Mackinac Island for our honeymoon, and were moving into our apartment in Ft. Wayne, Indiana on Tuesday. Ann continued her college education at the Ft. Wayne campus of Indiana University, and eventually earned her master's degree in elementary education. Here's a quick recap of my career with Auto-Owners:

1970: Auditor-Engineer, Minnesota

1971: Underwriter, Lansing Branch Underwriting Branch

1972: Special Agent, (Marketing Rep.) Northern Indiana Territory

1980: Manager, Market Development

1982: Regional Vice President of the White Bear Lake Branch

1988: Vice President of the Sales Department

1991: Senior Vice President for the Property and Casualty Marketing Department

1992: Senior Vice President for the Marketing Department

1995: Company director

1999: Executive Vice President

2004: CEO

2006: Chairman and CEO

People ask me why I have stayed with Auto-Owners all these years. First, let me say that I did leave the company for a few months in 1976. I quickly discovered that the grass *was not* greener on the other side of the fence! I took a position with another employer, only to find I had made a BIG MISTAKE!! I was blessed to be able to return to Auto-Owners shortly thereafter.

The reason I've been with Auto-Owners all these years is simple—the company was living by its 10 core values when I arrived, even though they were not specifically articulated back then, and we live by those same 10 values today. Those core values—Honesty, Hard Work, Prudence, Loyalty, The Team, Relationships, Opportunity, The Customer, Stability and Consistency, and Profit—are the same values I grew up with in North Dakota. Those values are not only great values for a company, but also great values for you as a person.

I would like to conclude with one observation. There will always be another job that will pay you more than the one you have now, whatever it is. I have been offered jobs that came close to doubling my salary. When I look back at the companies from which those offers came, some of them are out of business, others have announced massive layoffs or are hanging on by a financial thread. Investing in your career is a lot like investing in your financial future—shooting for big bucks quickly always entails a much higher level of risk than patiently working your way up the staircase. I would say to anyone who is considering leaving Auto-Owners for another company, before you make your decision, compare the core values of Auto Owners with those actually lived by that other company. I cannot imagine any other company winning out.

Joe's Introduction

The first time I saw Roger Looyenga, he was not a happy man. It was at one of those hotel conference centers with cheap sound-permeable walls separating the various rooms. I was giving a talk for a Chamber of Commerce group, and had just had all 200+ of my participants standing up and doing a rowdy lion roar at the tops of their lungs. Roger was in the next room trying to conduct a meeting, and had come over to complain about the noise my group was making. I ignored him for as long as I could, but I finally had to call a break. We talked for a while, and he ended up inviting me to visit Lansing. In the years since, I have worked with Auto-Owners on a number of different projects, I have become an Auto-Owners customer, and I am now one of the company's biggest fans.

I've worked with many organizations across North America, and as a student of values and leadership I've studied many others. I personally do not know of another organization anywhere that is so crystal clear about what its core values are, and about its expectations for individual associates to live those values. While many organizations talk about putting people ahead of profits, Auto-Owners is one of the few that really walks that talk. And belying the old aphorism that nice guys finish last, I believe that Auto-Owners has achieved its incredible success over the years precisely because so many nice people work there.

It has been a special privilege working with Roger and the rest of the Auto-Owners leadership team. In the course of our work together, I've been able to speak to associates and groups of independent insurance agents in each of the states the company serves, to create a curriculum on the company's ten core values, and interview each of the senior officers as well as many others. If anything, I've learned more from working with your company than you all have learned from me. I have learned how important it is to be a "no problem" person, and how valuable that attitude can be in both my business and personal life. Most important, this relationship has given me the opportunity to get to know people I will always consider to be good friends. Finally, I would like to express my appreciation to friends and colleagues on the Values Coach team, and especially to Sally (also known as Miss Bonkers), the lovely woman who runs my office and shares my life.

THE FIRST STEP

Developing Your Personal Strengths and Character

The first thing a leader must work on is him- or herself; if you don't begin with a platform of authenticity and solid character, you're building your career on a foundation of sand.

Always take the stairs

In most airports, shopping malls, hotels or other public places, you will be faced with a choice: Do you take the stairs, or do you have yourself hoisted up on the elevator or escalator? Most people choose the easy way, the way that requires the least effort. They stand passively in line waiting to be inertly hauled up to the next level. Ironically, even as they stand in line waiting for the escalator or moving walkway to deposit them at their destination, they might be wishing that they had more time for exercise.

This book is about choices. More specifically, it is about choosing to take the stairs. Unlike at the airport or the shopping mall, in the world of work there is no easy and effortless route to success (I can assure you no escalator will get you into the executive suite at Auto-Owners!). No moving walkway will convey you to the achievement of your goals and the fulfillment of your dreams.

In life, taking the easy way (the escalator, the elevator, the moving walkway) almost always leads to under-achievement and frustration. The choices offered in this book are all variations on this theme: when faced with the decision of whether to take the stairs or to ride up on the escalator, you will always be better off taking the stairs.

Success begins with living your values

If I'm asked what it takes to build a successful company or what it takes to create a meaningful life, my answer is the same: It all begins with values. One of the things that makes me most proud of working at Auto-Owners is the fact that we (we—all of us) take values very seriously. When the officers set about to specifically identify the core values of this company, we did not ask the question, "What should our values be?" Instead, we asked the question, "What have our values always been?" There was virtually unanimous consensus around the ten values we identified as being core to our heritage. These values have made our company successful, and they are the foundation of a successful career within our company.

These ten values, which are included in the appendix, guide every decision we make, and direct every action we take. That is one of the main reasons that we've taken values so seriously, including having commissioned Joe to work with us on creating a multimedia training program for all associates based on our ten core values. The best way for you to be successful at Auto-Owners is for you to live our values, and this course will help you do that.

Not only that, these same values apply directly to your personal life. For example, if you are honest and loyal, if you are a team player who works hard and takes care of your customers (including your coworkers), then you will build a successful career and lay a solid financial foundation for your future. As another example, working through the course modules on loyalty and relationships will not only help you be more effective in your job, they will also help you cultivate stronger family relationships.

Most companies have values statements posted on the wall. Unfortunately, at some of those companies the values statement is little more than window dressing. That is certainly not the case at Auto-Owners. We don't just talk the values talk, we walk the values talk. And we expect all of our associates to do likewise. I encourage you to become very familiar with these values... about how you can live them not only while on the job, but in all aspects of your personal and family life.

A NOTE FROM JOE

This is Roger's book, but I will periodically insert some of my own comments, beginning with this one. In my work as a Values Coach, I've worked with many different organizations from across the country, and have studied a great many more. I fully agree with Roger's assessment. In my opinion, there are few (if any) companies in America that are more clear about their core values, and more firmly committed to living those values in both philosophy and practice.

As I write this, I've just returned from a speaking tour with Auto-Owners agents in several states, which also gave me the opportunity to visit branch offices. I used the opportunity to take an informal little poll—I asked a more-or-less random selection of associates to recite the ten core values of Auto-Owners. Now, before I tell you the results, I'll say that I've worked with companies where the CEO would not be able to recite the values statement without looking it up. Of the people I questioned at Auto-Owners, the average (the average!) was ten out of ten. People had their own way of remembering the core values, but they each remembered them. It says a lot for the company, and a lot for the people who work for the company.

It takes courage to take the first step

One of my favorite quotes on courage is by Ralph Waldo Emerson, who said, "Do the thing you fear and the death of the fear is certain." Procrastination is usually an unwillingness to do something that you're afraid to do. We see it in our business all the time, don't we? People in marketing and sales who limit their potential success because they allow fear of rejection to keep them from making the calls that would create that success. The longer they procrastinate, the harder it is for them to get unstuck. At the extreme, they can end up being virtually paralyzed with fear.

Brian Tracy wrote a great little book titled *Eat That Frog* with advice for overcoming procrastination. The title is a play on the old saying that if you eat a live frog first thing in the morning, nothing worse will happen all day. Not having had the personal experience of eating a live frog first thing in the morning (or at any other time of the day), I'll have to take Tracy's word for it!

But I do believe his overall advice is right on target. If you "eat your live frog" first thing by tackling your most important, most daunting task before doing anything else, the rest of your day will be a breeze and you will be highly productive.

Tracy also says that if you have two frogs to eat, you should eat the ugliest one first—in other words, tackle the most difficult job first. He also said that if you must eat a frog, it really doesn't pay to sit there and stare at it. You just need to do it.

Each step leads to the next

I once saw a T-shirt that read, "Life is not a dress rehearsal." I imagine the person wearing the shirt meant to say that since you don't get to do your life all over again, you'd better get as much out of it as you can on this go-round. I'd have to say I agree with that.

But in one important respect, life *is* a dress rehearsal. Here's what I mean by that: Whatever you are doing today, and the way you are doing what you do today, in a very important way is your dress rehearsal for tomorrow. Let's say, for example, your goal is to be promoted into management. How you choose to "rehearse" for that job will both determine how successful you are at getting the job in the first place, and set the stage for how effectively you perform in that job once you've been given the opportunity.

On the one hand, you can begin to act "as if" you already have the desired position by being more proactive and showing more initiative, by being a positive team player, and by doing all the other things that others look for in a manager. On the other hand, when problems arise you can wait around and tell yourself things like, "If only I had a management title, I could do something about that problem."

People who act "as if" they already have the job tend to act their way into the opportunities they desire. People who moan that they would do something "if only" someone gave them the opportunity, usually spend the rest of their lives waiting. People who act "as if" they have the opportunity in front of them, and the resources they need will be available if they ask, get a lot more done and are much more successful—and they rarely find themselves saying "if only."

To grow means leaving your comfort zone

Helen Keller said that life is a daring adventure or it is nothing at all. One of the most important choices you make in your life is whether you live in the adventure zone, or strive to stay safe and secure in your comfort zone. Almost by definition, to go on an adventure requires a degree of uncertainty, risk, and discomfort. As my co-author Joe Tye likes to say, if you want to experience a sunrise in the Grand Canyon, you have to sleep on the cold ground. And while you almost certainly won't be bitten by a snake or a scorpion, you still must be prepared for that remote possibility.

That's a pretty good metaphor for the adventurous life: if you want to go to faraway and exotic places, you'll have to be willing to carry a heavier pack and face the possibility of difficulty along the way. But once you reach the mountaintop or the trail's end (or wherever your favorite adventure metaphor might lead you), you'll look back and know it was worth whatever pain it took for you to get there. So be willing to take risks, but then do all you can to prepare for the adventure and to mitigate whatever risks you might expect to see.

I'm sure you've seen one of those winding staircases where you cannot see the top step from the bottom. That's another good metaphor for seeing your life as an adventure. You have to be willing to take that first step, even though you can't see just exactly where it will lead. You need to have faith there is a worthy destination around the corner, have the courage to take that first step, and the determination to keep walking until you reach your goal.

Although we don't usually phrase it this way, organizations must also grow and adapt, which means leaving their corporate comfort zones. At Auto-Owners, our core value of Stability and Consistency does not mean that we don't change; quite to the contrary. We need to accept change, encourage change, and embrace change; status quo cannot be our measure of success or we will be left behind. Paradoxically, one of the ways that we can assure stability and consistency in the big picture is by being ahead of the curve when it comes to change—by changing because we see the need to change, and not waiting to change because we are forced by outside circumstances.

A NOTE FROM JOE

In my presentations to Auto-Owners independent agents during our regional meetings, I always point out that the only genuine empowerment is self-empowerment, and that the only people who can be empowered by others are those who have first empowered themselves to accept that power. One of the tools I share is *The Self-Empowerment Pledge: Seven Simple Promises That Will Change Your Life*. This Pledge is reproduced below.

As you read each of the seven promises (promises that you make to yourself), ask yourself this question: "If I really believed and acted upon these promises would I be in a better position personally, professionally, financially, spiritually, and in any other dimension of my life five years from now?" If your answer is yes (and if you're being honest with yourself, the answer will be yes), simply repeat each day's promise to yourself at least four times. As the promises sink in, you will find yourself cultivating a more positive attitude and a commitment to take the actions needed for you to achieve your goals and dreams.

THE SELF-EMPOWERMENT PLEDGE:
SEVEN SIMPLE PROMISES THAT WILL CHANGE YOUR LIFE

Monday's Promise: Responsibility

I will take complete responsibility for my health, my happiness, my success, and my life, and will not blame others for my problems or predicaments.

Tuesday's Promise: Accountability

I will not allow low self-esteem, self-limiting beliefs, or the negativity of others to prevent me from achieving my authentic goals and from becoming the person I am meant to be.

Wednesday's Promise: Determination

I will do the things I'm afraid to do, but which I know should be done. Sometimes this will mean asking for help to do that which I cannot do by myself.

Thursday's Promise: Contribution

I will earn the help I need in advance by helping other people now, and repay the help I receive by serving others later.

Friday's Promise: Resilience

I will face rejection and failure with courage, awareness, and perseverance, making these experiences the platform for future acceptance and success.

Saturday's Promise: Perspective

I will have faith that, though I might not understand why adversity happens, by my conscious choice I can find strength, compassion, and grace through my trials.

Sunday's Promise: Faith

My faith and my gratitude for all that I have been blessed with will shine through in my attitudes and in my actions.

I once received a call from an insurance agent who substantially increased his income simply by taking to heart Wednesday's Promise on Determination (he told me that if the world was fair, he'd be paying me a commission on his vastly increased earnings, but then reminded me that in my talk I had made the point the world is not always fair, so I would have to settle for just a thank you!). Whatever the problems you are facing, whatever the goals you are chasing, one or more of these promises will help you achieve success by empowering yourself—to use Roger's metaphor, by choosing to take the stairs.

You have to know when to stand tough

Any time you hear someone cite a statistic to the effect that most start-up companies fail, remind yourself it's simply not true. The fact is businesses do not fail—owners quit. For every business that ran into a wall and failed (i.e.

the owners quit), there's another business somewhere that ran into that same wall, but the owners found a way to go over, under, around or through that wall. They didn't roll over—they stood tough and fought a good fight, and today they have a successful business to show for their efforts.

There's a line from an old Kenny Rogers song that goes: "You've got to know when to hold 'em and know when to fold 'em." There's a real art to it, no doubt, but it's my impression that most people have a tendency to fold 'em much too soon, and that if they'd just stand tough and keep hammering away, they'd eventually break through whatever obstacles appear to be in their way. An important part of creating your own solid personal foundation is cultivating the strength of character needed to persevere through obstacles and setbacks—and to develop it *before* you need it.

You might have read the book by Harold Kushner titled *When Bad Things Happen to Good People*. Bad things *do* happen to good people. In fact, it's really just a matter of time before bad things happen to everyone. And when they do, you have the choice: Will you roll over and give in, or will you stand tough and fight it out?

Preparation is an investment in success

Being a Boy Scout was one of the most formative experiences of my youth, and the Scout Motto—Be Prepared—has stayed with me ever since. Here is the entire saying, taken from the 1908 handbook *Scouting for Boys* by Robert Baden-Powell and Elleke Boehmer:

> Be prepared in mind and body. Be prepared so you will know the right thing to do at the right time. Think out beforehand any accident or situation that might occur.

At Auto-Owners, much of my time each week is spent in meetings. I've found that there's a fairly direct correlation between how well I've prepared for a particular meeting and how productive that meeting is. I've also found a correlation between how well-prepared I am and how much I enjoy being a part of that meeting.

Abraham Lincoln said if he had eight hours to cut down a tree, he would spend six of those hours sharpening his ax. That's probably a pretty good proportion. If I have an important meeting that I expect to last one hour, and I spend three or four hours preparing for it, I usually feel confident going into the meeting, have a productive outcome, and enjoy myself in the process.

On the other hand, if I ever find myself getting bored, frustrated, or angry during a meeting, more often than not the root cause is I haven't adequately prepared. Even in my personal life, if I find myself worried or anxious, chances are it's because I don't feel like I'm prepared for something that might be looming in my immediate future.

Here's a suggestion for you. Pick a time every day that you can take a few minutes and ask yourself this question: "Am I prepared for everything that I expect to happen tomorrow?" I find the best time for me to ask myself that question is shortly after lunch. That way, if my answer is "no," then I'll have time to think about what I might not be ready for, and to do what I need to do in order to be ready.

Communication is an essential professional skill

Communication, or a lack thereof, is one of the most serious problems in any organization. And the faster and bigger an organization grows, the more difficult it is to maintain effective communication. That's why at Auto-Owners we have so many different mechanisms in place to assure that we're effectively communicating. But mechanisms and systems and media are no better than the people behind them. Communication is ultimately about people—people communicate with people. I believe there are two key elements for people communicating with people.

First, real communication means something of substance is being conveyed. Two people standing around the water cooler or the coffee pot spreading gossip are not communicating, they are just chattering. Real communication means knowing what you are talking about, thinking before you open your mouth, and understanding how what you say is likely to influence your listeners.

Second, real communication is a two-way street. It means paying attention to how (or whether) your message is being received, and then listening for feedback (which might be nonverbal). For example, a manager conducting a performance appraisal needs to make sure that the person whose performance is being reviewed truly understands what is being said, and that they are both clear on what is to be done as a follow-up. If you are not really listening, if it's just one-way expression, you're not really communicating, you're just talking to yourself. Going the other way, it means keeping your supervisor informed of important issues, the status of projects, and potential areas for improvement. It means asking for feedback as to how you can improve your performance. It also means knowing when to *not* communicate; once a decision has been made, get behind it and help make it work, don't second-guess it.

I've learned that the best communication is immediate and continuous. This basic rule of communication can be applied in both your business and personal life. Why is it that 300 people would be willing to stand in line at Disney World for 18 minutes on a day with 98-degree temperature and 106-percent humidity and think they had a great experience—and yet stand in line at another amusement park for two minutes and are ready to kill?

The answer is Disney knows the value of immediate and continuous communication. First, when you walk to the back of the line they communicate immediately with a sign telling you what the expected waiting time will be. Then, as you work your way toward the front of the line they continue to update you on the expected wait time from where you are; you might even be entertained by Disney characters while you wait. Before you even get on the ride, you already think you have had a great experience.

The most successful people are those who communicate best. The most successful businesses are those that communicate best. For example, let's assume you walk into a very busy restaurant. Which restaurant will be most successful? The one where the hostess greets you immediately and lets you know the approximate wait time (immediate communication) and offers you a seat in the lounge (continuous communication), or the one where you almost have to make a scene in order to be acknowledged by the wait staff (non-communication).

I've given talks to our claims representatives and made the following statement: "It is better to tell an insured that you will look at their loss in three days than not to tell them anything and show up in one day. It is important that you begin by determining expectations." Immediate communication allows the parties to agree on an acceptable timeframe. Three days might be acceptable if someone has had an automobile accident and has another car, but totally unacceptable if their house has burned down. Whether the mutual agreement is three days, one day, or three hours, it's all about showing respect for the time of our customers.

I believe a high percentage of personal or business relationships fail due to a failure of communication. People need the attention that comes from communication. Sometimes that communication only needs to be a few words—thank you; you're welcome; I'm sorry; I love you—said sincerely and said often. The right communication can heal, soothe, or keep a relationship from fracturing—both in business and personally.

A light heart makes it easier to take the stairs two at a time

A survey conducted by the Accountemps company in 1995 found that 90% of senior executives believe that having a good sense of humor is important for anyone desiring to reach senior management. Similar studies have shown that a good sense of humor is an important attribute for sales success. I haven't seen a study on this, but I imagine the same conclusion would be reached about having a sense of humor and being a great parent. Perhaps most important, smiling, laughing, and having a lighthearted approach to life is good for your health.

There are, of course, times when you need to be serious, but even in the most difficult of circumstances (and sometimes especially at those times) the ability to get people to lighten up and laugh is the mark of a real leader. People who are frightened and angry often do stupid things, and you cannot remain frightened and angry for very long if you're laughing.

Ironically, for many of us (especially those of us in the insurance business!) it's easier to be serious than it is to be humorous and light-hearted. That's why lightening up is often the "take the stairs" approach. There are lots of things you can do to cultivate your funny bone. As just one example, you can read more of the things that make you laugh (such as the humor sections in *Reader's Digest*, or collections of *Calvin and Hobbes* and *The Far Side* cartoons). If you come across a good one, please send it my way!

People have a choice of having a sense of humor or being like an old stuffed shirt. I believe people like to smile and laugh. When they do, they feel better and become more comfortable in their setting. Over the years I have participated in many meetings. If the person leading the meeting is gruff and lacks any sense of humor, the meeting becomes reserved and people hesitate to participate. When this happens the only creative thinking, if any, is done by the gruff leader of the meeting.

On the other hand, when the person leading the meeting has a smile, offers a little light humor, people want to join in. They are then more willing to offer suggestions and not be afraid to speak their mind. For example, our RC (rate committee) meetings used to be very serious and humorless. People were reluctant to offer ideas. Today RC meetings are still serious, but with a light and open atmosphere where humorous remarks are thrown in from time to time. I think some people have a more natural sense of humor than others. However, everyone can smile and interject a few light words. It is only a matter of choice. If you encourage something, you get more of it. If you discourage something, you get less of it. Make the choice of encouraging a sense of humor in others by having one yourself.

Bob Farrell has been a speaker for Auto-Owners events and most of us have heard his memorable message, "Give 'em the Pickle!" In his book of that title, Bob says: "A person rarely succeeds in anything, unless they have fun doing it." Insuring people against loss is a serious business, but that doesn't mean we can't lighten up and have fun doing it.

Once you start up the stairs, don't turn back

As I said in the introduction, one of my most positive experiences growing up was participating in Boy Scouts. I got to within one merit badge of obtaining my Eagle Scout, which was swimming. It wasn't that I didn't know how to swim. The Mandan swimming pool was closed the summer I wanted to get that last merit badge, and by the time the next year rolled around I thought I was too old for the Boy Scouts (something to do with my interest in girls and cars).

If I could do it over again, I would have stayed active in scouting for another year and earned my Eagle Scout. Looking back, I feel like a runner who dropped out of a marathon within sight of the finish line. Any track coach would have told me what I should have done: Imagine a tape several yards beyond the real finish line and run through that one. That's making the commitment to finish, instead of taking it *almost* all the way.

How about you? Are you committed to finishing what you start? Or will you let secondary distractions take your eye off the finish line that really matters in your work and in your life?

Boy Scouts was my first real leadership experience; it taught me that before you can be an effective leader, you must know how to be a good follower. And being a good follower begins with treating people with respect—especially your leaders. People follow people they know, like, trust and respect. I did not always agree with those who were in charge, but I always showed them the greatest respect. Today, scouting continues to be an outstanding organization for the development of boys into young men. I would urge all parents to encourage their sons and daughters to get involved in scouting or other team activities such as 4-H, music, sports, and student government so that they can begin learning some of the skills that will be required as they achieve leadership positions in adulthood.

Put in the extra effort

You have a choice to work hard or slack off. You also have a choice of activity only, or activity followed by accomplishment. I feel there is a direct correlation between working hard followed by accomplishment and personal satisfaction. We all have a need for positive recognition. To earn recognition we must work to accomplish something that will be recognized. I think everyone would say they want to be perfect. It is safe to say we will never be perfect. But there's no reason why we can't work toward that admirable goal.

A retired Auto-Owners Chairman and CEO, Max Tanner, said that to him, hard work meant working one additional highly concentrated hour at the end of each work day. The approximately 250 hours per year he was willing to invest was an important part of the difference between his having been a good manager and having become a great executive.

Lifelong learning is a key step to success

At a functional level, there is no practical difference between someone who knows how to read, but doesn't ever do it, and the person who is illiterate. I would take that one step farther and say there's barely a difference between someone who knows how to read, but only reads for entertainment, and the person who can't read at all. If you spent all those years learning how to read, and then all you do with that knowledge is read junk novels, gossip columns, and the sports pages, you might as well be illiterate. In my book, all of that education is going to waste.

It's often been said leaders are readers. I can tell you that's certainly the case at Auto-Owners. I'm quite confident in saying the Officers of our company are all readers. They read the trade press to stay on top of what's going on in our industry, and they read nonfiction literature to broaden their understanding of this business in particular, and of leadership principles in general.

You might have heard the computer acronym GIGO for "garbage in, garbage out." The same thing holds true for the human brain: the more intelligently you make choices about what you allow into your mind, the more intelligent you will be when it comes to making the choices and taking the actions that define the future course of your career and your life. Many times a day, you make a choice between the intellectual equivalent of eating a candy bar or eating a carrot.

Every evening when I get home, I have to make this choice: Am I going to plop down in front of the TV set, or am I going to read a book that is mentally nourishing? I know sitting there soaking in the violence, sensationalism, and commercialism that defines most of what's on television is like putting garbage into my head. On the other hand, reading a book (or listening to an audio program) on leadership, personal motivation, history or business is filling my head with information and ideas that can help me be more effective in my work. I find it also gives me the inspiration to put information and ideas to work.

Here's something else I find, another paradox if you will. No matter how tired and burned out I might feel when I get home, if I can force myself to go for a walk or a run, I return with more energy. That makes it easier for me to pick up a book that requires thinking, instead of wasting my time in a state of mental-neutral.

One last thing: I'm not saying you shouldn't ever entertain yourself with a good novel, or follow your favorite sports team in the newspapers. I do both. And I enjoy it all the more because it's a special treat, a nice break for when I'm not doing more serious reading.

Making the Right Choices

Every day and in many different ways we make choices that, while perhaps seeming to be insignificant at the time, add up to huge changes in direction and destination, for better or worse.

Be your best

When one of our sons graduated from college, I gave him a list of "be" statements I knew would help him as he continued his journey through life. The same statements are foundational to your success, both in your work here at Auto-Owners, and in your own journey on the path of life. Each of these "be" statements represents a choice, a choice you make each and every day, many times a day—in fact, every time you speak, every time you act. Here are the "be" statements I gave to my son—with a bit of thought on your part, you can come up with many more, can't you?

Be Honest: Everything but everything starts with honesty. It takes a long time to build character and a good reputation and only one dishonest act to lose it all.

Be Humble: There's a saying that goes, "People don't care how much you know until they know you care about them." Humility is an essential element of making a genuine connection with other human beings. Open-minded humility (a willingness to acknowledge you don't know everything, and being willing to learn from others) is also the foundation of creative thinking.

Be a Servant Leader: Motivational speaker Zig Ziglar has often said: "You can have everything in life you want if you just help enough other people get what they want." To me, that really captures the essence of servant leadership; it's not about achieving your goals, but rather working with other people to accomplish shared goals.

Be Your Best: You get the best out of life by putting your best into life. You really do reap what you sow. And every day, every hour, you make the choice whether or not to be your best—whether to take the stairs or the elevator.

Choose to have a positive attitude

If you've ever walked through the front door of the Auto-Owners headquarters building, you've probably been greeted by Diane Hogan. Diane might have bad days (everyone does), but you'd never know it by the warm and cheerful smile with which she greets every associate and visitor. She makes the choice, every single day, to be positive and cheerful (no matter what might be going on inside). And every single day, you have the same choice to make.

It's obviously difficult to make that choice on the days when it's gloomy on the outside and even gloomier on the inside. But here's the interesting thing. If, on the days when you're anxious and depressed, you go ahead and make a choice to be cheerful anyway, two wonderful things happen. First, before very long acting cheerful causes you to become cheerful, because you cannot sustain incompatible physical and emotional states for more than an hour or so. Second, as you work your way into being more positive and more enthusiastic, you attract other positive and enthusiastic people into your sphere. I've found once this happens, those other people very often can help you fix whatever problem it was that had you down in the first place.

I always cringe when I hear someone refer to another person as an "overachiever" or a "Pollyanna," as if there is something wrong with wanting to accomplish a lot, or with trying to see the positive side of life and wanting to make the world a better place. In my book, those are good things. I think we need more Pollyannas in our world, and fewer Dilberts. Pollyanna was always looking for the best in other people and wanted them to be happy. Dilbert, on the other hand, looks for the flaws in other people and rejoices when they fall on their faces. Pollyanna went out of her way to help people. Dilbert goes out of his way to make sure he's never asked to help. Pollyanna was a winner. Dilbert is a loser.

A NOTE FROM JOE

I refer to people who are chronically negative and constantly complaining as "pickle-suckers," because they always look like they have a sour pickle stuck in their mouths. I'm on a personal quest to eradicate toxic emotional negativity from the workplace environment. If you are a member of the BMW (bitching, moaning, and whining) Club; if you are in the habit of pointing fingers instead of looking in the mirror when things go wrong; or if you enjoy hanging around the water cooler spreading gossip, I doubt you'll have much of a future with Auto-Owners (or with any other good company for that matter).

I say this for two reasons. First, pickle-suckers are bad for business. They alienate customers and drag down morale. You know from your own experience, and behavioral researchers have proven through scientific experiment, that emotions are contagious. If you're in the habit of bringing your bad moods and negative attitudes to work with you, it probably won't be too long before you're invited to seek employment with the competition.

Second, as Daniel Goleman says in his book *Social Intelligence: The New Science of Human Relationships:* "Nourishing relationships have a beneficial impact on our health, while toxic ones can act like slow poison in our bodies." I'm certain that the leadership team at Auto-Owners feels a strong obligation to protect their associates from the deleterious effects of toxic emotional negativity in the workplace, to shield them from the pickle-suckers who suck the energy out of everyone they come into contact with.

I hope you'll join me in this quest—beginning by working to eradicate your own toxic emotional negativity (we all have it). Believe me when I say it will be one of the finest things you ever do for yourself. And it's simple (though not always easy). Just take The Pickle Pledge, printed below. It will change your life. I know it has changed mine, and I've seen it work in the lives of many others.

> I will turn every complaint into either a blessing or a constructive suggestion. By taking The Pickle Pledge, I am promising myself that I will no longer waste my time and energy on criticizing and complaining, nor will I commiserate with those who steal my energy with their criticizing and complaining.

Be a positive can-do thinker

Joe likes to make the distinction between positive thinking and wishful thinking. Positive thinking, he says, is expecting something and working to make it happen; wishful thinking is hoping for something and waiting for someone else to make it happen. Positive thinkers change the world; wishful thinkers get run over by change in the world.

Early in my career at Auto-Owners, I weighed 190 pounds, smoked a pack of cigarettes a day, and was in terrible physical shape. One night, Ann and I were watching the news on TV when results of a marathon (26.2 miles) run that day were announced. "Next year, I'm going to run in that race," I said. Ann looked at me as if I'd said I was going to walk across the English Channel. Then she laughed at me. Not with me, at me. I don't know about you, but I personally find being laughed at to be a great source of motivation.

The next morning I had to make a choice. Was I engaged in positive thinking or wishful thinking? On the way to the car, I dumped my entire supply of cigarettes into the garbage can. On the way home after work that day, I stopped at a sporting goods store and bought a pair of running shoes. Later on that evening, I went for a short, slow, and painful run. I ran every day for the next year. Those runs got progressively longer, faster, and more enjoyable.

One year after telling Ann I was going to run in a marathon, and having her laugh at me, I completed the race in three hours and 20 minutes. Through the power of positive thinking, I kept my promise. After crossing the finish line, I told Ann I'd never run another marathon. That's another promise I've kept!

Erase the words "I can't" from your vocabulary

Any time you hear yourself uttering those toxic two words "I can't," remind yourself this is probably a lie. In all likelihood, the truth is you really can, and what you are *really* saying is you don't want to, it won't be easy, or some other excuse. In most situations, a more truthful statement would be something like this: "I can, but first I need to (fill in the blank with whatever action is necessary to get you started on whatever it is)." This changes your focus from anchors (the things holding you back) to actions (the thing you must do in order to move forward). It also alters your mindset from disempowered victim to self-empowered winner.

Focusing on what you *can* do, instead of what you *can't* do, is a key first step in the goal-setting and achievement process. The statement "I can, but first I need to [fill in the blank]" helps you identify and prioritize the actions that you must take in order to reach your ultimate destination. For example, if your goal is to earn a CPCU, the steps will include contacting our education and training department, applying for acceptance with the CPCU Society, obtaining (and studying!) your books, then taking (and passing!) the exam.

Henry Ford once said, "Whether you think you can or you think you can't, you're right." And he's right! Always remember: If your goal is authentic, you *can* achieve that goal, though there might be a lot of other things that you need to do first.

Associate with positive people and avoid negative people

Read any parenting self-help book and you'll be advised to pay attention to who your kids are hanging around with, their so-called peer group. Well, it's not only kids who are influenced by their peers. In fact, sociologists tell us the people we choose to relate to—what they call our reference group—is probably the single most powerful factor influencing our attitudes and our decisions. So it's very important you pay attention to who you hang around with.

If your choice of a reference group is people who are negative and pessimistic, then over time you yourself will become negative and pessimistic. It might happen so slowly you don't even notice it happening, but it's virtually inevitable you will eventually take on characteristics common to your reference group. On the other hand, if your choice of a reference group is positive and optimistic people, those qualities will inevitably rub off on you as well.

The first thing I'd encourage you to do is avoid being part of a reference group of cynical, pessimistic, and negative people. If you're with a group and they start complaining, finger-pointing, or rumor-mongering, quickly make your exit. Then make it a point to never serve as a negative influence on others by engaging in these socially-toxic behaviors. The late Jerry Wilson, a professional speaker, said it best: "When you come into contact with people who have a negative attitude—RUN!"

The second thing I'd encourage you to do is consciously seek out positive and optimistic people to serve as part of your reference group. If you are making a genuine effort to improve yourself and your circumstances in life, I think you'll be surprised at how ready people are to help you. In fact, one thing I've discovered within Auto-Owners, and among the agents we serve, is the more successful somebody is, the more willing they are to help others become successful. All you have to do is ask.

Be prudent in making your choices

One of Auto-Owners ten core values is prudence—and prudence should be one of your personal and family core values as well. As a company, being prudent in our decision-making has allowed us to grow the business at a sustainable rate, to avoid cutbacks and layoffs during difficult times, and to avoid the serious mistakes that have bedeviled many other companies in our industry.

We live in a world in which being prudent means swimming against the current. In our materialistic society and advertising-driven economy, it takes real strength of character to make prudent decisions. Far too many people are not showing that strength. Too many people are not adequately saving for retirement, but somehow finding the money to pay for cable TV and other such luxuries. Too many people are not investing in their own education because they don't think they have time, yet somehow finding the time to watch television three or four hours a day (that is the national average, according to A.C. Nielsen). The best way for you to lay a solid foundation for your future is for you to make prudent decisions about how you're spending your time and your money in the present.

Use your time wisely

You have probably heard about the Pareto Principle, the famous 80-20 rule. This says in a typical sphere of life, 80% of the outcomes are created by only 20% of the inputs or activities. For example, 20% of Americans are responsible for 80% of health-care costs; for the typical business, 20% of customers generate 80% of sales; and for the typical salesperson, 20% of his or her time is directed into the activities that generate 80% of their revenue, with the other 80% spent on paperwork, meetings, coffee breaks, and other activities that don't have much revenue-generating potential.

The Pareto Principle is a statistical observation, a generalized tendency—not an immutable law of the universe. By changing the way you use your time, you can go from being an 80-20 person to being a 60-40 person, devoting 40 percent of your time on key priorities, rather than the 20 percent the average person devotes. The potential leverage is incredible. As just one example, if someone in commissioned sales were to increase the proportion of his or her time spent on prospecting and referral generation from 20 percent to 40 percent, it could result in *doubling* that individual's income—and with no less expenditure of time overall.

Every day, every hour, how we choose to invest our time defines the sort of results we will achieve. The choice is often between doing meaningful and productive work or doing what Don Jones, author of *The Better Way Agency Manual* calls BROMT work—boring, routine, ordinary, mundane and tedious. Obviously, there will always be work of that sort that needs to be done, but Auto-Owners has invested heavily in efficiency-enhancing automation so that, as much as possible, our people can invest their time in the more productive and rewarding aspects of their jobs. This includes serving customers, building relationships, and bringing in new business. We are, after all, in business to write business.

Make sure you have the right priorities

I often hear people talking about the difficulties they have balancing the various dimensions of their work life and their life outside of work, and I have struggled with this myself throughout my career. Here are two guidelines that I find helpful, and believe that you'll find helpful as well.

The first is from Mary Kay Ash, founder of Mary Kay Cosmetics. Mary Kay would tell her beauty consultants their priorities should be God first, family second, and career third. I agree. It is a matter of knowing what really matters, and (in the words of motivational speaker Anthony Robbins) making sure that you make the main thing the main thing.

The second is from leadership expert James A. Autry, who in his book *Love and Profit: The Art of Caring Leadership* says asking how to balance your personal life and your work life is the wrong question. The right question is how do you *integrate* your personal life and your work life? Asking this question can help you live your life more seamlessly, and not feel so much like you are juggling lots of separate little boxes. If you don't prioritize, you will end up randomizing.

A NOTE FROM JOE

I have a little poster in my office that reads "The One Big YES Requires Lots of Little No's." It is there to serve as a constant reminder that for me to achieve my big goals, I will have to forego lots of little diversions. It will be the same for you. As Roger says, being prudent means saving for the future *before* you spend for today, investing in your education *before* you spend time on entertaining yourself.

See your job description as a floor, not as a ceiling

Like virtually every other company, we have job descriptions at Auto-Owners. And, like virtually every other company, there is not always a strong correlation between what the job description requires and what they actually do in the course of a day. In fact, you might get the impression "other activities as delegated by the boss" is the most important line in our job descriptions!

One of the things I've noticed over the years is that the people who become superstars see their job description as a floor, not as a ceiling. Here's what I mean by that. People who think of the job description as a ceiling are constantly saying things like "that's not my job" or "not my department." For them, the job description places limita tions on what they expect of themselves, and upon what they are willing to give of themselves. Perhaps without even being aware of it, they also place a ceiling on their potential for career advancement.

People who see the job description as a floor, on the other hand, are willing to do what needs to be done, whether or not that work is technically part of their job description. When asked to do something that's not an officially-assigned duty, they don't respond with "not my job," but rather with "no problem" (assuming, of course, they know how to do what's being asked of them, or that they can get help and pick it up quickly).

Be grateful for the blessings of your life

Every Sunday morning, there's a lady sitting in her wheelchair in the front row of our church. She can't stand, and even if she could, she would only be about three feet tall. She has a disabling bone disease. She can break ribs just by coughing. But that doesn't stop her from singing.

I think about that lady whenever I hear somebody complaining about something, or if I catch myself doing it. Whatever it is that's being complained about seems pretty insignificant in comparison to her. If that lady can still smile and sing as a way of expressing her gratitude for being alive and for sitting in the front row at church, what can you or I possibly have to complain about?

That's another fundamental life choice, isn't it? No matter what happens to us, we can choose to be grateful for the blessings of our lives, or we can choose to be resentful for the things that we have not (yet) been blessed with. One thing I've observed over the years is that the choice we make, either grateful or resentful, has very little to do with outer circumstances and everything to do with our inner attitudes.

One person complains about having to park at the farthest end of the shopping mall parking lot; another is grateful for the opportunity to walk outside (and for having the legs to take that walk). One person complains about having too much work to do while the person at the very next desk is grateful for having work to do. You cannot simultaneously be grateful and resentful. Over time, gratitude is far more rewarding, in every sense of the word, than resentment.

Never give up

I almost did not finish the marathon I told you about earlier. At 20 miles, I ran into "the wall," the physical and emotional barricade that almost every marathoner has experienced. Although you can't see it with the eye, it's as real as the brick and mortar of an office building. "That's it," I told Ann, who had been riding alongside me on her bicycle the entire way. "I can't make it any farther. I'm quitting."

Before I could even slow down, Ann jammed the front wheel of her bike right up against my rear end. "No way, Roger!" she exclaimed. "For the past year, I've put up with you whining about your aching muscles, with late dinners, and everything else so you could train for this race. And now you're going to finish it!" And for the next 6 miles, she kept that bicycle wheel so close to me that if I'd stopped, I'd have been run over. Needless to say, I finished the race.

There's a key lesson here. To be a finisher does not necessarily mean you finish all by yourself. In fact, sometimes the only way you can prevent yourself from quitting is to have someone else help you across the finish line. That's a key reason that The Team is one of our core values at Auto-Owners. You're more likely to finish your race when you have the team working with you, or on occasion pushing you from behind.

See yourself as a winner, never as a victim

During my career at Auto-Owners, I've seen many examples of how one person can make a Big Difference. I've seen a marketing rep come into a "loser" territory and in very little time transform it into a real winner. I've also seen the reverse—a new marketing rep given a "winner" territory and before long, turn it into a struggling territory. Everything else was the same—same products, same prices, same agents. What made the Big Difference was the attitude of that one marketing rep, and his or her willingness to go to work. The person who has a victim mindset will inevitably under-perform the person who has a winner mindset.

It reminds me of the story of the two little boys at Christmas. The "empty glass" boy was given a roomful of toys and cried because he wanted even more of them. The "full glass" boy was given a roomful of horse manure, and was thrilled because he figured that must mean there's a pony around somewhere. The difference between being a winner or being a victim is, more than anything, state of mind—and the willingness to roll up your sleeves and go find that pony.

Be proactive

Years ago, Auto-Owners Vice President and Superintendent of Agencies A. Lynn Minzey coined the phrase "Ask them to buy." It's a timeless phrase with as much meaning today as when he first used it. "Ask them to buy" is the foundation of another Auto-Owners slogan, "In business to write business." We write a lot more business when we proactively ask people to buy rather than when we sit back and wait for people to call. If you have read *The 7 Habits of Highly Effective People,* you know that "be proactive" is the first of the seven habits described by Stephen Covey in that book.

There are usually questions you need to ask before you ask for the business. For the insurance agent, asking about a customer's family and lifestyle comes before asking that customer to buy a life insurance policy. For a teenage boy, asking a girl whether she likes to dance might come before asking her out to the prom. Minzey was reminding us not to stop with the introductory questions, but to forge ahead and ask for the sale, ask for the date, ask that closing question.

This principle has a much broader application in life. You'll be successful to the extent you're clear about what you want, and are willing to ask for it. This is what Jack Canfield and Mark Victor Hansen call The Aladdin Factor in their book of the same title: asking the right question of the right person at the right time.

Make a good impression

You've probably heard the term "business casual" used to describe a dress code that lies somewhere between the crisp blue suits and starched white shirts of IBM, and the sandals and cut-offs they wear at Apple Computer. There is obviously a wide range of apparel between these two extremes, and just as obviously there are times when each is most appropriate.

When you're standing in front of your dresser trying to decide whether to pull out dress shoes, running shoes, or flip-flops, remember this: You have only one chance to make a good first impression. Remember this also: you never know who you might meet in your travels. Here are several rules of thumb I offer for deciding where to fall on the continuum between business or casual:

Whatever you choose to wear, make sure you present yourself professionally. For example, at work your business dress should be clean and nicely pressed, and your shoes should be shined. Away from work, if you decide to wear blue jeans, don't choose the pair with holes in the knees; put on a sharp polo shirt (one with the Auto-Owners logo on it!) instead of a grubby T-shirt. Clothes might not make the man or woman, but they say a lot about him or her.

The look on your face might be the most important part of your wardrobe. If you're in the habit of wearing a friendly smile wherever you go, you'll make a much better first impression than you will if you look like you've got a lemon slice in your mouth.

Watch your language. Most people are put off by profanity, complaining, and other forms of verbal negativity. This sort of talk conveys a lack of professionalism, and people take you less seriously if they don't think you're professional.

First impressions are important—they make a lasting impression on the person perceiving them. Taking the stairs means making sure you take that first step in a way that leaves a positive first impression.

Never take the easy way out

The book *Insurance for Dummies* is available at the Auto-Owners Logo Shop. It's an excellent consumer guide, written by Jack Hungelmann, CIC, CPCU. Jack is an independent insurance agent in Edina, Minnesota and an Auto-Owners representative. I'm going to quote a full paragraph from Jack's book on buying insurance the wrong way, because it captures some of the most significant problems we at Auto-Owners want to assist our agents to help their customers avoid:

Most people buy insurance the wrong way. First, they buy it like a commodity—on price alone. Then, they let whoever answered the phone and gave them the quote be their agent, without any knowledge of that person's skill level. What they end up with, usually, is a cheap price... for the wrong coverage. Not to mention a less-skilled agent than they could have had for the same price. What they end up with, ultimately, are claims that are either denied or underpaid because of wrong coverage. They end up with significant financial losses. They end up with an insurance program that didn't do the job they hired it to do.

For the customer who takes it seriously, obtaining insurance is a two-step process. First, they need to find the best agent, and then obtain the most appropriate and effective coverage. That is the "take the stairs" approach. Unfortunately, all too many people take the "escalator" approach by simply making a few phone calls to find the cheapest price for what they think they need (which might not, in fact, be what they really need).

You might recall the old television ad for an oil filter (Fram) that goes, "You can pay me now or you can pay me later." The message was a bit of preventive maintenance now could avoid a big repair bill later. It's a paradox that people who choose to do it the right way and take the stairs now end up having things go more smoothly and easily for them later. People who take the easy way out to avoid a bit of work and expense in the short run usually end up paying a big price down the road.

Be an energy faucet, not an energy drain

Have you ever been in a room when someone with a scowl on their face and negative attitude radiating from every pore walked in and sucked the energy right out of the room? That person is an energy drain. I've also heard people like that referred to as energy vampires, which might be even more accurate. It's a form of theft, really, as if someone is pick-pocketing energy from everyone else in the room. They're stealing from their coworkers, and they're stealing from their organization. And to top it off, they don't even do anything with the energy they've stolen; after the theft, they're still the same old negative and bitter people.

On the other hand, I'm sure you've had the experience of someone walking into a room with a smile and a positive attitude, giving everyone else in that room a shot of energy. These people are energy faucets. My co-author Joe Tye calls people like this Spark Plugs because they take a bit of their own energy and turn it into a spark that zaps positive energy into the people around them.

This is a critically important choice for you in your professional career. I've never seen an energy drain climb very high up the ladder of success. Nobody wants to elevate someone who brings people down. Successful people are always high-energy people, and they are always anxious to share their energy with the people around them. But even more important than professional success, it's hard for me to imagine an energy drain being very happy in their personal life.

Here are three energy techniques every successful person I know uses, one way or another. The first is regular physical exercise. It doesn't have to be a full-blown workout; just walking faster through the parking lot and taking the stairs instead of the elevator will help you have more energy. Strange as it might seem, you gain energy by using it.

The second is a commitment to positive thinking and optimistic expectations. If you are a negative and pessimistic person, you're naturally going to have low energy, because it's hard to motivate yourself to put energy into something you expect to go badly.

Finally, successful people use little rituals to get themselves fired up on their low-energy days (and we all have them). Doing the Lion Roar (the noise-making exercise Joe was doing with his audience when we first met, as he mentioned in his introductory comments) is a great little ritual for blasting your way out of the energy doldrums. You simply visualize whatever it is holding you back and roar at it, the way a lion might roar at a mouse.

Honor your need for spiritual growth

It's been said that we are not human beings who have spiritual experiences, we are spiritual beings who have human experiences. It's easy to forget this in the world of business, where we tend to focus on things that can be categorized, counted, and accumulated. In his book *Love and Work: A Manager's Search for Meaning,* James A. Autry wrote:

> I believe that much spiritual growth is possible through the doing of business because of the simple fact that the doing of business requires interaction with our fellow human beings, and within those interactions are vast possibilities for spiritual connection and growth.

Autry also said one of our great challenges is to create a working environment where people can grow personally and spiritually as well as professionally. One of our core values at Auto-Owners is Opportunity for Associates. I believe this includes the opportunity for personal and spiritual growth, and not just professional advancement.

We recently had a dinner function with Auto-Owners officers, claims managers, and marketing reps. There were over 200 people in attendance. Prior to dinner being served, I went to the podium and asked Jeff Harrold to give a blessing; I hadn't planned to do this, and frankly don't remember it ever having been done in the past. I've had more people come up to me or write me saying how much they appreciated this break in tradition. I would encourage anyone who is not practicing their faith to find a church, synagogue, mosque, or other religious community that strengthens faith and helps put action into that faith. For me, this has been a powerfully life-enhancing step.

Making choices means accepting tradeoffs

I'm sure you've heard the saying there is no free lunch. Well, it's the same when it comes to making choices. There is always a tradeoff. To say "yes" to one thing almost always means saying "no" to something else. That's one of the reasons why it's so important for you to think carefully about the choices you make.

At Auto-Owners, we've made the choice to market our products exclusively through the independent agency system. This is not because of a sentimental attachment to that system (though there are many independent insurance agents we consider to be great friends). It's because we believe the independent agency system does the best job of serving our policyholders.

There are tradeoffs associated with this choice. We have declared we will not compete with independent agencies by hiring a direct sales force, by marketing via the Internet, or in some other way. In the short run, at least, we could probably make more money by expanding the channels through which we market our products. We are willing to accept that tradeoff, and to forgo the additional money we might be able to make, because we're more interested in long-term relationships than we are in short-term profits.

Throughout your life, you will face many choices. You'll make much better choices, and come to regret those choices much less often, if you will be honest with yourself about the tradeoffs you are making at the same time, and if you will give priority to long-term success rather than to short-term gain.

Working with the Team

In the complex and fast-changing world of today, you cannot succeed unless you master the art and skill of working with and motivating the members of a team.

Be part of the team

People do not work *for* the Auto-Owners Insurance Company. They are *a part of* the company. Our company is a team. You'll never hear someone say something like, "I work for a team." Rather they say, "I'm *part of* the team." It's the same with our company. Like any great organization, Auto-Owners is nothing more than a group of people working together as a team to serve its customers, and to support each other.

When we were refining the ten core values of Auto-

Owners, we had a spirited discussion about whether we should call this one "Teamwork" or just "The Team." We elected "The Team," because in our view, this reflects something bigger than simply a group of people getting the work done. A group of people can come together to get a job done who don't even like each other. To the outside observer, they look like a team, but they're not—they're just engaged in teamwork. When we speak of "the team," we mean a group of people (associates, agents, customers) who work well together because they know, like, trust, and respect one another. We also mean they buy-in, they take ownership for the values of the company, for our mission of providing super outstanding service for our customers (associates, agents, policyholders), and for doing whatever we can to help the other members of our team.

Auto-Owners is really a team of teams

One of Auto-Owners core values is The Team. A commitment to the "team" influences every aspect of our business. I often say that none of us individually are as smart as all of us together. That philosophy, and the commitment to act upon it, is a great part of the strength of our company. As just one example, the senior officers meet for lunch every day they're not traveling. During those meetings, we discuss important decisions that must be made. People are quite vocal about sharing their thoughts and opinions, but in the end it's a team decision, and once the decision has been made we work as a team to see it through.

The team concept recognizes we all have weaknesses and we all have strengths. When people come together with their strengths and weaknesses, the team becomes strong because all the weaknesses of the individuals are overcome by the strengths of others. I remember coming to the senior officer team with what I thought was the best marketing idea ever developed for our company. It turned out to be a good idea, but it became an even better idea after others gave their input. This is why the major company decisions are made in a team-thinking environment.

Auto-Owners is really a team of teams. In your job, whatever it is, you are a member of one or more teams. Being part of a team really brings with it two essential responsibilities. The first is to be your best and to do your best. I say that out of genuine concern for you as a person. In his beautiful little book *The Prophet*, Kahlil Gibran said that "work is love made visible." And when everyone on a team is doing their best work, it is a beautiful thing indeed. The second responsibility is to help others on the team be their best and do their best. At one time or another, we are all in the position to support, coach, mentor, or simply carry water for a fellow associate. That's the best way to build a team, and to bring down the "silo walls" that often impede communication between teams.

Keep the team growing to keep it going

Auto-Owners core value of Stability and Consistency does not mean we don't want to grow—far from it. In fact, growing the business is one of the key ways we are able to honor one of our other core values—Opportunity for Associates (not to mention Profit, another of our ten core values). As we say in one of our slogans, we are "in business to write business," and we are not at all shy about sending that message to the independent agents who represent our products in the marketplace. We have also opened service offices in several new states in recent years, and will continue searching for attractive opportunities to grow in this way.

We rely on our associates to help spark this growth in many ways. First, by maintaining our solid productivity edge when compared to our competitors, we are able to help our agents write more business with us. Second, when we provide Super Outstanding Service to our customers, they are more likely to do more business with us, and to encourage others to do the same. Finally, as we continue to grow, we will need to add dedicated and hardworking new associates. Historically, our best people have come via referrals from associates, including in many instances family members. So if you know someone who seems like an Auto-Owners type of person, send them our way; we want to speak with them!

Deal with conflicts by taking the high road

At some point, we are all placed in situations that require us to make a decision between values that are in conflict. Throughout the history of corporate free enterprise, there have been some shocking and well-publicized failures caused by a lack of integrity. This dishonesty and corruption were choices made by people (not corporations) where individuals consciously decided to be dishonest and corrupt. In most of those situations people were placed in positions where they had to choose between two

ROGER LOOYENGA

62

values that we hold dear at Auto-Owners: Honesty and Loyalty. At Auto-Owners, this should be a no-brainer: Honesty always trumps Loyalty, with no exceptions, ever. For example, if a manager were ever to ask you to show your loyalty to him or her by performing a dishonest act, there should be no question about which value you would honor: HONESTY.

There are other situations, however, where the picture is not so clear cut. Here at Auto-Owners, for example, there could well come a time when you have to make a choice between Opportunity (the chance to move ahead in your career or to relocate geographically) and Stability and Consistency (your desire to stay in a job situation and work climate in which you are comfortable, or to not disrupt your family situation). Chances are no one else can tell you what to do in such a situation, but the more clear you are about your priorities in life the more certain it is you will make the right decision. I believe that if you commit yourself to always taking the high road (i.e. take the stairs), you will always make the right decision.

It's also important to know when something superficially appears to require a choice between values is actually a false dichotomy (if you don't know what this word means, you have a choice, don't you?). For example, at Auto-Owners there will never be a situation where anyone must choose between people OR the bottom line. People always come first at Auto-Owners. We're confident if we always put people first, then profit will take care of itself. And I'm certain you will find the same thing is true in your own career—and in managing your household. Over time, it always pays to put people first.

Be consistent and predictable

I can remember working with an associate that one day could be the nicest person in the world and the next day be demeaning and nasty. People began to avoid him, not knowing what side of his personality they might encounter—the Dr. Jekyll or the Mr. Hyde. If they had an important subject for discussion or a decision that needed to be made, they would wait until they thought he would be in a reasonably good mood. As you might imagine, it was the cause of much uncertainty and inconsistency.

It is important for leaders to be reasonably consistent and predictable. I think it is better for someone to have an abrasive personality consistently rather than one that seesaws between nasty and nice. At least people know what to expect when they approach that person. People do not like inconsistency. Here's a simple but effective habit for you to get into: each morning before you leave for work, remind yourself of who you are and of what you want people to see in you during the course of that day. Then strive to be that person all day long. If you've decided to be a sourpuss, at least be consistent about it.

But why would anyone choose an abrasive personality, or choose to be a sourpuss, when they can just as readily decide to be pleasant and get positive energy in return from other people? Once you develop the habits, it doesn't take any more energy to be cheerful, positive and optimistic than it does to be grumpy, negative, and pessimistic. To mix the pickle metaphors of two people who have been speakers at Auto-Owners events (Bob Farrell and Joe Tye), when customers want the pickle, give 'em the pickle, but when it comes to your own attitude, get that pickle out of your mouth!

This principle of consistency also holds true in the sales arena. Todd Duncan wrote in his book *Killing the Sale: 10 Fatal Mistakes Salespeople Make and How to Avoid Them:* "The bottom line is that unwavering sales success is maintained by consistency." He says when you act in a consistent manner, you get consistent reactions from your customers, which in turn leads to consistent sales results.

Lift people up instead of taking them down

I call this the elevator principle: you can either lift people up or you can take them down. When I think about the associates and the independent agents who have been successful at Auto-Owners, they all seem to have permanently punched the "up" buttons on their mental elevators. They consistently seek to lift up the people around them. They look for opportunities to catch people doing things right and to compliment them for it; they encourage people to pursue their ideas, and to progress in their careers. They seem to have a radar that zeroes in on people who are struggling, then go out of their way to give those people a lift.

Then there are the people whose mental elevator buttons are stuck in the "down" position. They seem to thrive on knocking others down. They tease and belittle people, and then gossip behind their backs. They make fun of their ideas, and tell them that they'll never work. "Down" people take a perverse joy at seeing someone else fall on

their face, and then stand to the side making snide remarks as that person struggles to get back up.

One of our core values at Auto-Owners is Opportunity for our Associates. If you're an "up" person, there will
be lots of opportunities for you to move up in our company. And the more you help lift up your coworkers, the
more of those opportunities will come your way.

Be a people person, not a things person

Auto-Owners is different from many (perhaps most)
other companies in that our most important decisions are
not financially driven. We don't have to worry about pleas-
ing Wall Street with our most recent quarterly results, and
we don't make decisions with an eye as to how they might
affect our bottom line. The first parameter we consider in
every important decision is the impact on people—associates, agents, and policyholders (i.e. our customers), and on
the community at large.

Here's an example: at many (perhaps most) other companies someone scheduled to begin work on December 28
would probably be asked to postpone their start date until
January 2. At Auto-Owners, someone scheduled to start
on January 2 would probably be asked to move up his or

her start date to December 28 so they could be included in our Christmas bonus for that year.

A number of years ago, Marsha Sinetar wrote a book titled *Do What You Love, the Money Will Follow.* At Auto-Owners, we practice a variation on this theme. We believe if our people are allowed to do what they love to do, and they do what they do with passion, then profit will take care of itself; that's why Profit is last in our list of core values. That is also why at Auto-Owners we practice what we call "reverse job-posting." Instead of posting open jobs the way most other companies do, we offer our associates the opportunity to login their preferences for their ideal next job in their ideal office location; then we consider them when a job meeting those specifications opens. It's just one more way that we put people first.

Put your heart into the work

Henry Ford once complained that when he hired a man for a pair of hands to work on the assembly line, those hands came attached to a head and a heart. He wanted people to work, but not to think or feel. He didn't understand that people can't leave their creative talents and their personal lives at the door when they come to work.

At Auto-Owners Insurance, we're glad you come complete with a head and a heart! We want to hear your ideas, and we want you to bring your heart to work. We want to see you smile and we want to hear you laugh. We hope you'll make lots of friends while you're here, and you will consider some of these people to be among your best friends. We'd like to see pictures of your family posted in your work area, and have a chance to meet your children. If any of your relatives are looking for a great place to work, we hope you will steer them in our direction.

We also know that having a heart sometimes means having your heart broken. We want to be here for you in those times when things aren't going so well. When we say one of our core values is loyalty, we don't just mean we'll do everything possible to protect your job (although for more than 90 years we've been successful at doing that). To me, loyalty also means standing beside someone during their tough times, being there for them through the tears as well as being there for the laughter. And at Auto-Owners, we want to be there for you in those times as well.

We also expect you to respect the fact your fellow associates here at Auto-Owners have heads and hearts. While we want to be here for you during your difficult times, we don't want to see you dragging down other people with petty complaining. A big part of being a mature and considerate adult is knowing when to share your problems and ask for help, and when to just buck up, smile, and get on with your life without "venting" on others.

Exchange the spotlight for a floodlight

In the years after the Chicago Bulls drafted Michael Jordan, he set the basketball court on fire, winning scoring titles, MVP awards, slam dunk contests, and in the process becoming a household name. But when playoff time rolled around, the Bulls were home watching the games on TV. What's wrong with this picture? The spotlight was shining on Michael Jordan while his teammates toiled in the shadows. And one great player will never beat a team of five good players.

It was only when coach Phil Jackson exchanged the spotlight for a floodlight, and other players like Scottie Pippen and B.J. Armstrong stepped out of Michael Jordan's shadow, that the Bulls went on to become America's dominant basketball team, winning six-of-ten titles during the 1990s. When Coach Jackson took this "floodlight" coaching philosophy with him to the Los Angeles Lakers, they won the national title the next three years running.

Auto-Owners is a floodlight sort of company. We value the team, and don't place much stock in the idea of lone ranger superstars. To be successful in this organization, you have to have a pretty tight rein on your ego, and be genuinely interested in helping other people be successful. You must be willing to share the floodlight, not try to hog the spotlight all to yourself. But through the paradox of service that Joe described earlier, when you shine that light on others it reflects back even more brightly on you, because at Auto-Owners valuing the team also means valuing team players.

Demand excellence and don't tolerate mediocrity

In any organization, corporate culture is defined by two things: what you expect, and what you tolerate. In many organizations, there's a big gap between stated expectations, and what is actually perceived by workers and customers in the field.

We've all had the experience of dealing with companies that have mission statements promising that "customers come first," but whose employees make us feel like our needs are at the bottom of their priority list. In large measure, that's because managers in those organizations tolerate attitudes and behaviors that are inconsistent with their stated expectations. And over time, what you tolerate will always outweigh what you say you expect.

One of the strengths that has made Auto-Owners so successful over the years is that, when it comes to the things that really matter, we don't just *expect* performance, we *demand* it. Most corporations expected their people to act with integrity; the word is often right there in their values statements. But some corporate leaders are willing to tolerate substantial variations from what you or I would consider to be acting with integrity. That gap eventually brings the company down, and harms a lot of people in the process.

At Auto-Owners, we don't just expect honesty (our first core value), we demand it. We don't tolerate dishonesty of any kind or at any level, because we know that little lies inevitably lead to big lies, and big lies inevitably cause big problems. And we're "The 'No Problem' People®."

Loyalty is more than mere tenure

Loyalty is one of our ten core values at Auto-Owners. Our ability to earn the loyalty of associates, agents, and customers is a key reason we're growing and thriving, through hard markets and soft markets. Over the years, we have been in difficult business situations where many other companies would have laid people off, but we made the tough choice to honor our value of loyalty instead . For example, I remember when I became the Regional Vice President in Minnesota, most of the underwriters and processors were completely caught up with their work by noon. We took that opportunity to call our agents asking them how we could write more business, we cross trained and studied insurance training courses. Eventually the market hardened, and we were much better prepared to take on the rush of new business.

We work very hard to earn that loyalty, and have had to make some tough choices along the way. For example, our declaration of total commitment to the independent insurance agency system means we will not pursue other potentially lucrative marketing avenues for our products. And we're especially proud of the fact that in 90 years of operation, we've never had a layoff, because our commitment to the security of our associates forecloses taking the easy way out during times of financial difficulty.

We hope for, and quite frankly expect, loyalty in return. And when I use the term loyalty, I mean it in a proactive sense. True loyalty is more than mere tenure. Simply showing up for work year after year is not loyalty, it's just putting in your time. Genuine loyalty means investing in your own skills and education so you can make a contribution to your coworkers and to the company. It means going the extra mile to anticipate and take care of customer problems. It means bringing a smile to work, and leaving your gripes and complaints in the parking lot. As former Auto-Owners Chairman and CEO Max Tanner used to say, "If you take care of the company, the company will take care of you."

One dimension of Auto-Owners commitment to loyalty is that, with only the rarest of exceptions, we exclusively promote from within. The people who are most likely to be honored with those promotions are those who've shown the type of proactive loyalty I described in the previous paragraph.

Being a Servant and Making a Contribution

It is an ancient paradox that those who are most thoroughly committed to serving others end up being the most effective leaders.

Choose to be a servant leader

When I'm asked about my leadership philosophy, I can summarize it in two words: servant leadership. If you want to be effective and successful as a leader, and certainly if you want to be a leader at Auto-Owners Insurance Company, you must first and foremost see yourself as a servant to those you presume to lead. As they climb the stairs, the best leaders are both looking ahead and looking behind; they are charting a course to the future, and reaching back to give a helping hand to those climbing behind them.

The first requirement of servant leadership is listening—*really* listening. Servant leaders pay attention not only to words, but also to the emotions behind those words; they seek to understand and to empathize. The second requirement is being concerned with getting the work done, and not with getting credit for the work being done; quite to the contrary, servant leaders are more interested in reflecting credit onto others than they are in taking it for themselves. The third requirement is a commitment to doing whatever it takes to serve customers and coworkers. In his book *The World's Most Powerful Leadership Principle: How to Become a Servant Leader,* James C. Hunter writes:

> Developing the skills of servant leadership is difficult work and comes with a price. Becoming a servant leader requires a great deal of motivation, feedback, and extended practice, as does any worthwhile discipline... To become a better leader, one must be willing and motivated to change and grow. To develop leadership skills, one must

be motivated to seek out and receive sometimes painful feedback from others so one can see oneself more clearly.

In other words, if you want to be an effective leader, you need to put your ego on ice and always promote and support others; recognize they may stand out above you. Doing this, you will gain the satisfaction of accomplishment and of seeing people grow. I once saw a great example of this at an Auto-Owners regional meeting. We had arrived at our hotel late in the evening, and the hotel staff had done a terrible job of preparing the room for our meeting the following morning. Herm Arends, who was then our CEO and Chairman, found a housekeepers closet, pulled out a vacuum cleaner, and vacuumed the carpet. Then he helped us arrange handouts. It is a lesson I have never forgotten, and a story that captures an important dimension of the heart of this company.

Servant leadership is at the heart of Super Outstanding Service

Since 1997 we have embarked upon a training program at Auto-Owners called SOS—Super Outstanding

Service. Numerous books, videotapes and DVDs have been developed on the subject of customer service excellence. Likewise there are just as many definitions of "outstanding service."

I think the best definition of "outstanding service" is this: How outstanding did the customer think the service was? Nothing more, nothing less. In other words, how the customer perceives service is the definition of excellence that really matters. If we think we're delivering great service, and the customer believes it's less than outstanding, then it is less than outstanding. In this respect, at least, the customer is always right.

I recall having read about a study in which two groups of students had to stand in line to check out library books. The clerk serving one group was friendly and cheerful, the clerk serving the second group was a surly grouch, but they were both equally slow and inefficient. The second time around each student group was paired with the same clerk, but this time the grumpy clerk was twice as fast as the friendly one. The students didn't even notice—they still rated the service as having been poor. I remember Herm Arends saying many times, "You can have the best dog food in the world, but if the dogs won't eat it, it isn't good dog food." That grouchy librarian probably thought she was delivering great service, but her opinion didn't matter in the slightest if the students thought it was terrible service.

Our goal at Auto-Owners is for every one of our customers to walk away from their service experience saying "WOW." They then tell their friends and neighbors, who tell their friends and neighbors, and the company continues to grow by word-of-mouth that is fueled by our SOS—Super Outstanding Service.

Build your momentum

There's an old adage that says if you're not growing, you're dying. I absolutely believe that to be true. Building a great business, having a successful career, and leading a meaningful life depends upon constantly giving yourself new goals and new challenges. It means raising the bar, just a little bit, every single day. If you've ever watched the high jump or the pole vault events in the Olympics, you know after an athlete has cleared a certain height, the bar is raised by another fraction of an inch. That's a great metaphor for life: success is achieved by fractions of inches day after day, not by one mighty leap all at once.

I hope you've seen the videotape of the presentation Jeff Harrold and I gave on *The Power of One*. In business and in life, it really is little things that make the big difference. Again, sports is a great metaphor: in almost every Olympic event, the difference between winning a gold medal and no medal is usually measured in tiny fractions. It's the runner who does a few extra laps after everyone else has called it a day who stands atop the platform to hear the performance of his or her national anthem.

What if each and every one of us were to do one additional thing every day to provide Super Outstanding Service? What if we all made the commitment to come in five minutes earlier so we're already rolling when the day starts? What if each day we would each make one additional phone call to ask how we could help an agent or a fellow associate? What if we each raised our own bar by the power of one, and then raised it again? Can you imagine how much more dynamic this organization would be?

One of the key reasons that Auto-Owners has been so successful over the years, and that we are able to offer so many opportunities and unparalleled job security to our associates, is we keep raising the bar, year after year.

Of course, companies don't really raise the bar, people do. And our future success—*your* future success—will be defined by our commitment to the power of one, and to continuously raising the bar of our expectations.

Do your work with passion

"If your heart is in your dream, no request is too extreme." I love that line from the classic Disney song *When You Wish upon a Star.* Big dreamers are people who are passionate about their dreams. They make those dreams come true by investing heart and soul into their accomplishment. Like forces of nature, passionate people are unstoppable. Their enthusiasm and commitment (both are characteristics of passionate people) drive them toward the achievement of their goals.

To be passionate does not necessarily mean you have to stand up on a chair and wave pom-poms. Some of the most passionate people I've ever known are actually quite reserved. Herm Arends, our now-retired Chairman and CEO, is passionate about his work, his family, and about life in general. When you first meet him, he comes across as being a pretty studious numbers guy (which he is), but you don't have to be around him very long before you begin to catch his contagious enthusiasm. That complementary blend of serious attention to the overall business and playful enthusiasm about the work itself is one of the things that makes Herm such an effective leader.

Here is a pretty good definition for the source of passion: *extravagant caring.* Passionate people really care! Passionate sports fans feel real pain when their teams lose, because they really care. Passionate salespeople go the extra mile to build relationships, because they really care. Passionate CSRs do whatever it takes to help customers, because they really care.

One of the things you can do to spark a higher level of passion in your life is to remind yourself that you really care—and then act like you do. There might be times where, as they say in AA, you have to fake it till you make it, but pretty soon caring will become second nature, as will the passion that springs from caring.

A NOTE FROM JOE

There is incredible wisdom built into the 12 steps of AA, and lots of snappy one-liners to back it up. One of my favorites is "fake it till you make it." It doesn't matter how you feel inside, if you *act* passionate, if you *act* like you care, your emotions will take their cue from your body language and facial expressions and you *will* become more passionate and you *will* care more.

Redefine your definition of the job

As I think about the people I've worked with over the years, they seem to fall into three general categories when it comes to how they view their work. First, there are those for whom work is a job: primarily the means to a paycheck and the other benefits that go along with having a job. For sure, they (hopefully!) enjoy the work and the people they work with, but their primary motivation is personal economics. People for whom the work is a job would be unlikely to take night school classes on their own time and expense in order to learn new skills.

The second category are those who see their work as a career. When you think of a career, you probably envision a series of jobs, with increasing levels of expectation and responsibility (and the financial rewards that accompany these new duties), but it's more than that. Seeing your work as a career also implies making investments in yourself—in your education, your relationships, and your commitment to doing excellent work. Something else: the focus of the person who is just performing a job is on getting the work done; the focus of someone with a career is on earning more work to do.

Finally, the third category is people who see their work not just as a job or a career, but as a calling. When I think of someone with a calling, musicians and doctors come to mind—people who seemed to know from the time they could walk what they wanted to become. But I've also met many people for whom insurance is more than a job or career. For them, helping people cope with the disasters and tragedies of life really is a calling. In Abraham Maslow's well-known hierarchy of needs, the highest human need is food, clothing and shelter. Second is protection and security—and that is what we insurance professionals give to our customers. That's a noble calling.

I think of an Auto-Owners agent who got a call from a client whose house had burned down. The man escaped the fire in his pajamas, but he lost everything else, including the wallet containing his cash and credit cards. Without a moment's hesitation, that agent withdrew $1,000 in cash and took it to his homeless customer so he could buy some clothes and check into a hotel while the paper-work started to be processed. That's seeing the work as a calling.

There's nothing wrong with seeing your work as a job or as a career. I'd say that most of the associates at Auto-Owners (as at most other companies) fall into one of these two categories, and that's just fine. But I will say people who also see the work as a calling—a calling to serve—tend to make more money in their jobs, and to go farther in their careers. Therefore, seeing an element of calling in your work can be a very wise choice, and a great investment in your future.

"No problem" really means "problem solved"

At Auto-Owners Insurance, we pride ourselves on being "The 'No Problem' People." But when we say "no problem," we aren't just saying "don't worry about it" the way a teenage kid might respond to the question of when he'll get around to mowing the lawn. What we are really saying is this: "*You* have a problem that *we* are going to make *our* problem; we are going to take ownership and resolve this problem for you, so you won't *need to* worry about it."

That's a pretty fundamental difference, isn't it? The teenage kid and the Auto-Owners associate are saying the same words, but they mean something totally different. When the teenager says "no problem," it probably comes across more like, "you have a problem—gee, that's too bad." When the Auto-Owners associate says no problem, it means "don't worry about this problem of yours, because I'm going to resolve it for you." In other words, "your problem becomes my problem and I am taking responsibility for fixing it."

Almost by definition, any time a customer calls us—whether it's an agent or an insured—that person has a problem. Our job is to fix that problem so quickly and completely that all the customer can say is WOW! That's what we mean by Super Outstanding Service.

Don't just patch problems, get to root causes and fix them

Someone once shared with me a copy of a letter an irate customer had sent to the CEO of a cereal company. It seems she had found a bug in a box of the company's cereal. The CEO replied he was shocked to hear this, since the company prided itself on its exacting quality standards. "To think a bug was able to enter our plant is most disturbing," he said, and enclosed a coupon for five free boxes of cereal to compensate her for "this unpleasant experience." On the back side of the CEO's letter, the lady found a Post-it Note in the CEO's handwriting that read: "Pat, please send this lady our bug letter."

Now, I think this letter was probably a joke—at least I hope it didn't really happen! But it does bring up an important point. At Auto-Owners, when we say "no problem," we don't just mean we'll take care of the immediate problem, the way that cereal company CEO got the unhappy customer off his back by sending her a letter and a coupon for 5 free boxes of cereal. To us, "no problem" means when a problem arises, as they will, we'll deal with that immediate problem and also take care of the underlying cause, to make sure it won't happen again.

Raymond Aaron is a successful entrepreneur and business coach in Canada. He often reminds people of this ultimate truth: Life means having problems. A good life is having new and interesting problems; a bad life is having the same old problems recycling themselves over and over again. In that sense, our approach to being "The 'No Problem' People" is also part of the formula for leading a productive, successful, and happy life.

When you are faced with a problem—with your job, your relationships, your finances, or anything else—make a commitment not to just deal with the symptoms of the problem, but to tackle the underlying cause. This will allow you to grow into new and more interesting problems, rather than facing the same old problems day after day.

Think like an owner, not like a renter

Have you ever checked the oil in a rental car? I haven't either. People who are renting something are naturally less likely to take care of it than people who are owners. Maybe that's why Vern Moulton decided to call our company Auto-Owners instead of calling it Auto-Renters!

Whether you are an owner or a renter extends beyond physical property; it's also a frame of mind. People who take mental ownership for something are much more committed than people who have the attitude they're just passing through. They are more likely to make an investment of time by doing great work on the job.

I sometimes think, in addition to giving people a job description, we should also give them a certificate of ownership for that job. But when it comes to your job at Auto-

Owners, you really don't need a certificate. It's *your* job, so just go ahead and take ownership for getting it done to the very best of your ability. Keep investing in yourself with ongoing education, work hard at developing solid relationships, go out of your way to be helpful—because those are the things that an owner would do.

Love is all you need

My favorite Bible chapter is 1 Corinthians 13. Within this chapter, Saint Paul speaks of the power of hope, faith, and love—and says that the greatest of these three is love. Love is a word we probably don't hear enough in the business world, because the greatest organizations are built on a foundation of love—love between people, love of achievement, love of the work itself.

One of the greatest human needs is to feel loved. Love is a gift that, given unconditionally, almost always is repaid in kind. But as Dr. Scott Peck noted in his book *The Road Less Traveled,* love is not just a gushy emotion; love is hard work. Love is putting yourself at the service of others, putting their needs before yours, working hard on their behalf, making sacrifices for their benefit. Love requires patience (showing self-control). Love requires kindness (to give attention, appreciation, and encouragement). Love requires humility (displaying an absence of pride, arrogance, or pretense). Love requires respect (treating people like they are important). Love requires selflessness (meeting the needs of others). Love requires forgiveness (letting go of resentment). Hard work indeed.

The Beatles had a lot to say about love that's directly applicable to our work at Auto-Owners. Like this: "There's nothing you can do that can't be done—all you need is love." And like this: "And in the end, the love you take is equal to the love you make."

I believe that one of the key factors in Auto-Owners success over the past 90 years has been that we put our hearts into our work, and we put our hearts into the service of the agents and customers we're privileged to support. In other words, we do a lot because we put a lot of love into what we do!

Walk the talk

In his book *Dig Your Well Before You're Thirsty*, Harvey Mackay says the acid test of effective networking is the answer to this question: How many people could you call at two in the morning if you had an emergency?

That's a good question, but I think this is a better one: How many people would have you on their list of people they could call at two in the morning if they had an emergency?

At Auto-Owners, we pride ourselves on being "The 'No Problem' People." If you walk that talk—if you really do help people take care of their problems, and do it cheerfully and effectively; a lot of the people you've helped will have *you* on their roster of "friends in need, friends indeed," of people they might call in the event of an emergency in the middle of the night. On the other hand, if you're one who stands aside and watches someone else take care of those problems, people aren't likely to think of you if they have that midnight crisis.

Here's an interesting paradox: If you're the kind of person that others think to call when they have a midnight emergency, you might on occasion lose a few hours of sleep, but you'll sleep a lot better knowing how many people think of you as "a friend indeed."

THE FIFTH STEP

Becoming a Leader

Leadership is not so much a set of activities as it is a state of mind—a commitment to continuously seek out ways to make a better world, and the determination to bring the changes needed to bring that world into being.

At Auto-Owners, honesty is not a choice

Would you do business with someone you cannot trust? Would you want to be working in the cubicle next to someone you cannot trust? Would you want to work for a company that could not be trusted with your job security, your health and retirement plans, and the quality of your workplace at the top of its priorities? I know my answer is "no" to these questions, and I hope your answer is the same. In the section just above, I commented that being honest is a choice, and it is. But the day an Auto-Owners associate chooses not to be honest will be that associate's last day. Auto-Owners puts trust in its people, and the company expects honesty in return.

Earning a reputation for honesty is a lot like climbing a mountain. The climb up is long and arduous—and one tiny misstep can cause you to come down quickly and catastrophically. We've seen over and over again how the dishonesty of a few people can destroy an entire company, and cause serious harm to the people who have relied on that company as employees, as customers, and as investors. At Auto-Owners, we have been climbing that mountain (talk about taking the stairs!) for more than 90 years, and we will not allow dishonesty on the part of anyone associated with this company—from the CEO to our newest hire—to jeopardize the reputation we have worked so hard to earn.

Honesty always begins with self-honesty, and deceiving others always begins with self-deception. Shakespeare wrote that if you are true to yourself, you'll never be false to anyone else. In the same way, as soon as you start deceiving yourself, it's only a matter of time before you're trying to deceive others as well.

The Auto-Owners Insurance Company has a zero-tolerance policy when it comes to dishonesty!

A NOTE FROM JOE

It says a lot about Auto-Owners Insurance that the company's first core value is Honesty. I truly believe that when you gain something by telling a lie, you lose something far more important than what you have gained. When you lose something as a result of telling the truth, you gain something far more valuable than what you have lost.

I invited Auto-Owners CEO Roger Looyenga to be a speaker at one of my seminars on values-based leadership. He shared the ten core values of Auto-Owners Insurance Company, giving specific examples of how each are reflected in the company's operating philosophy and corporate culture. During a discussion about tolerating failure and learning from mistakes, Roger described a situation in which an Auto-Owners associate had made a decision that cost the company many millions of dollars. "Was he fired?" asked one of the seminar participants. Roger said no.

The questioner was astonished, and asked, "If someone doesn't get fired for losing millions of dollars, what will they be fired for?" There was not a moment's hesitation in Roger's reply: "Being dishonest." The questioner persisted: "What if the dishonesty made the company millions of dollars? Would that make a difference?" Again, there was no hesitation in Roger's reply: "Absolutely not. For one thing, you cannot make money at Auto-Owners by being dishonest, because as soon as the transgression was discovered, we'd pay it back. Besides, we can recover from financial losses. But once a company has been tarnished with the stain of dishonesty, it's almost impossible to restore its good reputation."

Let your heart guide your head

We've all heard the saying, "he or she has a big heart." That is another way of saying that person considers others first in whatever they do. We have also heard the saying, "he or she has a big head." That's another way of saying that the person in question is probably thinking of him or herself first before they think of others.

Everything we do on this earth involves people. Everything! There isn't one action, one result, that doesn't involve a person. It therefore makes sense that all we do, starts first with the question, "How are other people affected?"

I have two guidelines for acting with heart first and head second. The first is to be completely honest with yourself. When you think about most of the scandals that have brought down powerful people in the worlds of politics, business, and religion, I'll bet that without exception the problem began when someone allowed a big head to overrule their heart, and they rationalized away what they should have known to be dishonest behavior.

And second, acting with heart first means placing yourself in the position of being a servant to others. Think again of those front-page scandals. In every single case the people involved were thinking only of themselves and their own interests—amassing personal wealth and gaining power over others. Had these people possessed a servant mindset, they never would have lied and cheated and stolen; and they would today have a lot more of the things they wanted in the first place, including respect, happiness, money, and in some cases their very freedom.

Here's something to think about: The more we serve others, the bigger our hearts will grow and the less others will think we have big heads. If you want to be successful in your career with Auto-Owners, this is the best advice I can give you: Be a servant. Serve your coworkers, serve the agents who represent our company, and serve the people we insure. But more than this, serve your family and serve your community. One thing I can promise you is that, to paraphrase Dr. Albert Schweitzer, the success you achieve in your career and the quality you experience in your life will be directly proportional to the opportunities you create to be of service to others.

Leadership at Auto-Owners is servant leadership

One thing that characterizes Auto-Owners is a commitment to servant leadership. People who are successful at Auto-Owners are successful precisely because they have invested time and energy in helping other people to be successful. They make it a priority to serve as coaches and mentors for others, even though they themselves have more responsibilities and more time commitments of their own as they progress in their careers.

In my view, being a servant leader and taking the stairs are absolutely complementary. People who are committed to serving others are willing to take the stairs, and people who take the stairs inevitably emerge as leaders. If you take nothing from this book other than to make a commitment to view yourself as a servant first and a leader (or leader in the making) second, then our time together will have been a real success.

Leadership is about people and relationships

By definition, leaders are people who lead other people. And how do you earn the right to call yourself a leader? By developing positive, nurturing, and empowering relationships with people. You cannot coach or mentor someone (two essential elements of real leadership) without entering into a relationship with that person. In his book *Indomitable Spirit: Life-Changing Lessons in Leadership* Chuck Ferguson wrote:

> Leadership isn't about a product. It isn't about a process. It's not the product you deliver, but the people you deal with. Products and services can pay the bills, but people build the greatness of your organization. And you deal with those exasperating, troubled, but utterly human souls by encouraging them. Inspiring them. Doing your best, whatever it takes, to help them do their best.

I can't think of a better prescription for being the sort of leader who is successful at Auto-Owners. If you're the type of person who encourages, inspires, and goes out of your way to help your coworkers do their best work, and become their best selves, you have a great future with our company.

Develop your strengths and rely on others to help you in your areas of weakness

As I've mentioned, turning your strengths into areas of brilliance is a much more productive personal strategy than trying to turn your weaknesses into strengths. Identify your strengths, which are those things that you are best at, and will make you the most happy, and develop those the best you can, and spend considerably less time working on your weaknesses. Then find people who have your weaknesses as their strengths and surround yourself with them. You are most likely to be successful when you are being authentic, and your strengths—those activities that bring you the greatest sense of personal joy and re ward—are a powerful guidepost leading you toward the authentic you.

As paradoxical as this might seem, trying to do everything yourself is often taking the easy way out. It's hard work (one of Auto-Owners ten core values) to find and work with people who complement your weaknesses with their strengths, but that is about as clear a definition of being a leader as you'll find.

If you want to write a book and writing is not one of your strengths, you're better off finding a coauthor to work on the writing, allowing you to focus on developing the core concepts and key points you want to make in that book. Of course, as I have learned in the process of creating this book, working with a coauthor means being willing to engage in give-and-take, to listen to opinions as well as give them. That, too, is a crucial element of teamwork and of leadership; honoring other people's strengths by being receptive to their thoughts and opinions.

Work to cultivate your leadership abilities

For Auto-Owners to be a consistently great company it will require leadership at every level of the organization. As my coauthor puts it, in today's complex and competitive world, we need leadership in every corner, not just in the corner office. If you want to develop your abilities as a leader, it begins by making a commitment to see yourself as a leader, and then working on developing the strengths that will make you a better leader.

I consider a leader to be a coach. A basketball coach doesn't need to be the best basketball player on the court, but does need to make sure each of the players are the best they can be. The coach will recognize some players are better on offense than on defense, and structure the game plan accordingly. Likewise the leader in an organization, regardless of his or her title, doesn't need to be the best at everything, but does need to make sure that each of the people on the team is working at their very best. The leader needs to be aware of his or her own strengths, and then help others uncover and cultivate their strengths.

If there is one key to success in life it is this one: Choose to surround yourself with people who complement your weaknesses and who let you build upon your strengths. For many years I worked extra hard in developing my weaknesses. The only result was I was frustrated by having stronger weaknesses. Over the years Auto-Owners has had CEOs who were genuine financial wizards and CEOs whose strengths were in sales and marketing. Rather than trying to turn their weaknesses into strengths, at the risk of becoming a jack of all trades and a master of none, in each case these CEOs have relied on the team to fill in for them in areas of their weakness, and rely upon them in the areas of their greatest strength.

I believe the best thing you can do to be a more effective leader is to figure out what your God-given strengths are, and then to work on developing those strengths. Working on your weaknesses might help you become better. Working on your strengths can help you become GREAT.

A NOTE FROM JOE

The distinction is often made between management and leadership. For example, it's been said that management is doing things right while leadership is doing the right thing. Here's my take: management is a job description, leadership is a life decision. Your boss can make you a manager by giving you a title and a job description, but that will not necessarily make you a leader. Being a leader means looking for opportunities to make things better, then taking the initiative to act upon those opportunities.

Leaders see the best in all situations

I'm sure you're familiar with the famous opening line of Charles Dickens' novel *A Tale of Two Cities:* "It was the best of times, it was the worst of times." I'm reminded of that line every time I'm involved in a conversation about soft markets and hard markets in the insurance business. In soft markets, there tends to be intense competition for market share, exerting downward pressure on pricing for premiums. In hard markets, a constrained supply of insurance products tends to drive prices up. Either market condition has its own special challenges.

So which is the best of times and which is the worst of times—hard markets or soft markets? At Auto-Owners, our answer is—"Yes." We make it the best of times, whether it's a hard market or a soft market. During soft markets we don't join the rush to slash prices in the hopes of buying market share with new policies that might not otherwise meet our quality standards. And in hard markets we don't stop writing business or increase our prices excessively, thereby driving away good customers. This consistency of practice helps us stay off the roller coaster that has gotten so many other insurance companies into trouble.

The same principle can help you in your career and in your personal life. When your attitudes and behaviors are anchored in core values, the way our company is anchored by our value of stability and consistency, it helps you stay off the emotional roller coaster. Instead of happiness being determined by outside forces, it's anchored by inner values, character, and overarching goals. Instead of panicking or getting depressed during times of difficulty, you take problems in stride and seek out the opportunities (for personal growth and learning, if nothing else) that these difficulties always bring in their wake. And when you're on a roll, you retain your spirit of humility and prudence. Whatever the world throws at you, choose to see the best of times, because in life you tend to find what you're looking for.

Leaders need to be visible and accessible

All of the senior officers at Auto-Owners answer their own telephones—we don't have our calls screened by secretaries. Anyone in the company can call my direct line and if I'm in the office I'll pick up the phone; if I'm not in the office, you'll get my personal voice mail and a prompt return call from me, not from an assistant. That is just one manifestation of the commitment of Auto-Owners leadership team to be visible and accessible.

Back in the early 1980s the book *In Search of Excellence* by Tom Peters and Bob Waterman outlined management practices of some of America's best-run companies. One of those practices was "management by walking around," or MBWA. This does not mean simply wandering around, coffee cup in hand, chatting with people. To deserve the name "management," MBWA means to connect with people, to ask meaningful questions, to listen carefully to their needs and concerns, and to leave people a bit more energized for the encounter. As leadership authority John C. Maxwell says, MBWA is not just breezing through an area, it's also taking time to connect the way the cars on a train are coupled together.

Leaders work on developing their charisma

One of the most famous studies in the field of organizational behavior was one conducted by Elton Mayo in the 1920s and '30s. In this study, the management of a factory made a series of small changes in the workplace to ascertain what would yield the greatest productivity. No matter what the researchers did, it seemed, productivity improved. In one of the most important findings of the study, it turned out the simple fact of being studied—of being made to feel important—encouraged people to work more productively. There is an important lesson for us as leaders. Letting people know we take them seriously, we appreciate their efforts, and we do indeed believe they are important to our success is a great way to encourage them to perform at their best. And that, in turn, is the essence of leadership charisma.

If you've attended one of my coauthor's *Spark Your*

Success sessions, you know this is how he defines charisma: the ability to make someone else feel special by being part of something important. He shares the advice of Mary Kay Ash (founder of the cosmetics company that bears her name) that whenever you speak with someone, you should visualize the letters MMFI stenciled on that person's forehead, standing for Make Me Feel Important. Since charisma, by this definition, is vital to becoming an effective leader, then it stands to reason we should all work on developing it.

Focus on other people

Recently, I overheard my wife, Ann, talking on the phone. As the conversation continued, I realized Ann kept the focus on the other person, and never once talked about her own issues or interests. She showed a genuine concern for what was happening in this other person's life—asking questions about her family and friends, her job, and her upcoming activities. I wondered how quickly the conversation would have ended if Ann had stopped showing interest in this person and instead shifted the focus onto herself. My guess is that it would have been a pretty short conversation.

In his book *How to Win Friends and Influence People,* Dale Carnegie wrote the most important sound a person can hear is his or her own name. By that, he meant people have a strong need for personal attention and recognition. This point was reinforced by psychologist Abraham Maslow, who in his famous "hierarchy of needs" identified recognition as being a powerfully important human need, and source of reward. As I said earlier, this is a great definition of leadership charisma—the ability to make other people feel important. You do that by keeping the focus on them and their needs, and not allowing it to shift back onto you.

Here is a simple rule that can help you be more effective at winning friends and influencing the people around you: I call it *The 3-2-1 Principle.* There are three letters in the word YOU, there are two letters in the word ME, and there is one letter in the word I. When you are with someone else, weigh that accordingly—make sure the conversation is two, or even three, times more about them than it is about you. The best way to do that is to ask questions. "Tell me about your kids; tell me how work is going; tell me what your plans are for the holidays." Ask people to tell you about themselves, and they'll leave the conversation thinking of you as a great communicator.

Leaders look out for others

Zig Ziglar says we all listen to the same radio station—WIIFM—What's In It For Me? He also says you can have just about anything you want in life if you'll just help enough other people get whatever it is they want. In the choice between those two perspectives—"What's in it for me?" or "How can I help you?"—real leaders always choose the latter. "How can I help you, how can I be of service?" is the mindset that lies at the heart of servant leadership.

The most effective and influential leaders, and the kind of people who are most likely to be successful at Auto-Owners, think first of how they can serve others, not of how others can serve them. They truly believe "no problem" means going out of their way to help other people solve their problems, even if it means putting more, and bigger, problems on their own lists of things that must be done.

During my years with Auto-Owners, I've known many fine leaders. Without exception, they were hard-working, busy people who had long to-do lists. And without exception, they never hesitated to add something else onto those already-extensive to-do lists if it would help a fellow associate, an agent, or customer. That's why they became leaders. That brings me again to the paradox of servant leadership. The best way—in fact the only way to become a leader is not by trying to become a leader; rather it is by committing yourself to being an effective servant. The reward of effective servanthood is leadership.

Everyone is a leader

Everyone is a leader at some time, but no one is a leader all the time. Experts in the field call this situational leadership; in different situations, different people emerge as leaders depending upon the needs of the time. The best organizations, including Auto-Owners, encourage this distribution of leadership responsibility.

Situational leadership works because people follow people who meet their needs. I remember in a group problem-solving exercise at the Center for Creative Leadership being appointed the leader by the group members. This was the problem we were given: A group was driving through a blinding snowstorm, hit a patch of ice and slid off the road. The moment before the car went into the ditch, the car's occupants saw the lights of a distant farmhouse. Everyone had winter clothes, and the car was equipped with flashlights, blankets, and other survival gear. So here was the question we had to answer: Do we stay in the car until morning or do we try and make it to the farmhouse?

Everyone in the group (other than me) said the answer was obvious—we should walk to the farmhouse, since it didn't appear to be that far away. But then I told them of my upbringing in North Dakota, where we would have these sorts of blinding snowstorms. Sometimes during a storm, I told them, a farmer would try walking from his house to the barn—a short walk he had made thousands of times in the past. Yet despite his total familiarity with the route, the farmer would disappear—and his frozen body would be found the following day. Becoming disoriented in the whiteout conditions of the storm, he had wandered around in circles and was unable to find his house again. After telling that story, I was appointed group leader for our discussion of the problem—not because of my position, but because of my special knowledge.

Something similar occurs at Auto-Owners rate committee meetings. As CEO, I conduct the meeting when I'm there, but I'm not always the meeting's leader. People know not to look to me for many of the answers, because there are other people in the room with more knowledge and expertise than me. My job is not to lead, it's to let those people take the lead. In his book *The 21 Irrefutable Laws of Leadership*, John C. Maxwell writes that the best leaders are people who raise up other leaders. Thus, one of the leader's key responsibilities is to recognize the strengths of others in the organizations, create opportunities for them to exercise those strengths in a leadership capacity, and then empower them to step into that leadership role.

Leadership is a game of momentum

One of the reasons that Stability and Consistency are among the ten core values of Auto-Owners is we appreciate the power of momentum. Rather than race ahead for a while, then slam on the breaks, we want to maintain steady and solid momentum forward. In life, as in business, you are either going forward or you're going backward. The important thing to realize, whether at the level of our company or at the level of your personal life, is it takes energy and stamina to reach the point where you have built up momentum.

Let's look at the history of Auto-Owners as an example. It took our company 71 years to reach $1 billion in premium income. It took ten years for us to reach the second billion, three years to reach the third billion, and 18 months to surpass the 4-billion-dollar mark. I've seen the same thing happen with the growth path of many insurance agencies, as well as the individual careers of insurance agents and Auto-Owners associates. I've seen it in my own life, and I'm sure you've seen it in yours. It takes time and energy to get the ball rolling, and to keep it rolling, but it's much more rewarding and much less exhausting than a start-and-stop existence.

Keep raising the bar

Certain types of fish will grow to fit the size of their habitat. Keep them in a small fish tank and they'll remain small fish. Put them in a giant aquarium and they'll become very big fish.

That's a great metaphor for personal growth and development. You will grow to meet the expectations you establish for yourself. If you don't expect very much, if you settle into a contented complacence once you've achieved those expectations, you won't grow very much, and you won't go very far. You will remain a little fish in a little pond.

On the other hand, if you keep raising the bar—keep pushing out the walls that define your own personal aquarium, so to speak—then you will continue to develop as a professional and grow as a person. You will also find yourself at the head of a growing school of "fish" following you, because people are naturally attracted to courageous boundary-expanders.

There is, of course, one key difference between you and the fish. Unlike the fish, once you find your nose bumping up against the aquarium glass, it is within your power to make it bigger. The fish is forever trapped within that little glass home; you are free to push out the boundaries, to expand your tank, or to escape it altogether.

So, what can you do to keep raising the bar? Well, I'm convinced that it's doing five percent more on lots of little things. For example, answering voice mail and email before you go home each day, and not allowing it to pile up. Making one extra phone call to find the right decision-maker, to ask for the sale, or to better serve the customer. And it's bringing your heart to work (and leaving your aching feet at home).

I also think you must keep raising the bar on your family front. Make a point of being there for your kids' soccer games. And keep raising the bar on yourself. Go for additional education and training, that higher level of certification. Take a woodworking class, or learn how to play golf. And make time for reading, thinking, and for just being with yourself.

That's how you grow as a person. That's also why we keep raising the bar at Auto-Owners. We know the only way we can grow as a company is if our associates continue to grow as professionals, and as people. It's a great challenge for you: How can you raise the bar this year, both in the personal and professional dimensions of your life?

Take the stairs

What does it mean to take the stairs? It means being true to core values instead of just going with the flow. When you are faced with a tough decision, taking the stairs means doing the right thing instead of doing the easy or expedient thing. When given the choice between serving others or indulging yourself, taking the stairs means being a servant.

Taking the stairs is harder than riding up on the escalator or the elevator. It might take you longer to get to the top. It requires that you separate yourself from the herd. But here's my promise: If you conscientiously and consistently make that choice, you will develop the strength of character, the personal discipline, and the leadership skills you need to be happy and successful in every dimension of your professional and personal lives. It is worth the effort.

A NOTE FROM JOE

As I've passed through O'Hare airport over the years, I've been conducting an informal research project. At each end of the underground tunnel that connects the B and C concourses of United Airlines, there is a very long staircase with an escalator on either side. For every one person who takes the stairs, more than 10,000 ride up on the escalator. This is a fitting metaphor for Roger's message in this book: If you make the commitment to always take the stairs in your work and in your life, you will be in rare company.

A final word on Auto-Owners future

Auto-Owners has been one of the most successful insurance companies in the United States. We are now one of America's 20 largest insurance companies and a member of the Fortune 500, all while operating in only one-half of the states (not including the most populous states of New York, California, or Texas). Our future success will depend upon how well we remember what has made us successful—our commitment to putting people first.

In this high-tech world, it is so easy to forget success does not depend upon having the right business model or the right technology—it depends on people. It is then easy to forget those little things people need. A sincere interest in who they are and what makes them tick, a friendly hello, a smile, a "thank you," an "I'm sorry." When people feel they are wanted, needed and appreciated, they will want to be part of the organization. If they don't feel these things, instead of being a team player they'll sit on the bench and be a spectator.

Our future, our success or failure, will depend on how well we take care of the people who are associated with us—our associates, our agents and our policyholders. How well we take care of people starts with all of these seemingly little things that really turn out to be very big things. When it comes to people, always take the stairs!

The Ten Core Values of Auto-Owners

As I mentioned at the beginning of this book, success at Auto-Owners begins and ends with values—and so does this book. When we were developing the training curriculum for Auto-Owners ten core values, we asked each of the senior officers to make a comment on one of these ten values. I've included these comments below. These are the values that we at Auto-Owners live by.

The First Core Value — Honesty

"Honesty is truly the cornerstone for everyone to have a less complicated and more joyful life. That is why honesty is so important to me. I do not want to work at having to remember what I told a person. Being honest, I (and all of us at Auto-Owners) have 'No Problem' providing consistent messages. We can use the energy we might use keeping 'stories' straight for productive activity. The best gift I can give to a fellow associate is a truthful, honest evaluation of performance. It is a gift because it shows I care enough to help the person grow. To be dishonest in many situations is to rob a person of the opportunity to learn and grow from honest, kind input."

> **Ron Simon,**
> *President*

The Second Core Value — Hard Work

"Hard work has always been part of that invisible something that is embedded in our Company's culture. You can just feel it and it fuels our success. Whether it is associates providing Super Outstanding Service, controlling expenses or developing themselves for future opportunities, hard work is front and center."

> **Ken Schroeder,**
> *Senior Vice President, Commercial Lines Underwriting*

The Third Core Value — Prudence

"Prudence does not mean being miserly, it means being wise. When we are prudent, we have the resources to make essential investments in people and capital, to be competitive in the marketplace, and to maintain loyalty to our associates and to our agents through the tough times as well as the good times.

Stuart Birn,
Senior Vice President, Secretary & General Counsel

The Fourth Core Value — Loyalty

"Loyalty is the essential ingredient in a successful business relationship, in a friendship, in a family—in short, in virtually every dimension of life and work. The old saying that a friend in need is a friend indeed is right on target, and our goal is that Auto-Owners will be an organization that is filled with friends indeed."

Jeff Harrold,
Executive Vice President

The Fifth Core Value — The Team

"A patchwork quilt is a great metaphor for the team at Auto-Owners. A quilt organizes many different patches of material, each with its own uniqueness, into a single unit that serves a useful purpose, while still allowing the individuality of each piece of fabric to stand out. And that is our goal at Auto-Owners—to foster a united organization that also honors the individuality of each associate."

Bob Buchanan,
Senior Vice President, Applications Development

The Sixth Core Value — Relationships

"Whether we are working with our agency customers, outside vendors, or working with each other, work is so much more pleasant when we have positive relationships with each other. If a group of people are gathered for a common cause, and the atmosphere is positive, chances are positive relationships are going to build. Here at Auto-Owners, we have many groups of people and many accomplishments we are working toward. The great thing is each of us also has the power to create that positive atmosphere. It doesn't matter what our position in the company is or what our background and skills are. When we choose to lead and create a positive atmosphere, others will join in and great relationships will form."

Dan Thelen,
Senior Vice President, Personnel

The Seventh Core Value — Opportunity

"The most important thing an associate can do to create opportunity is to focus on doing a good job in his or her current position. Through this performance, passion, and commitment to Auto-Owners, people will notice when an associate demonstrates readiness for another opportunity and respond accordingly."

Jeff Tagsold,
Senior Vice President, Personal Lines Underwriting

The Eighth Core Value — The Customer

"Our jobs are dependent on having CUSTOMERS to serve. The best way to attract and retain customers is to show them they are important to us. We do that by providing 'The Customer' with service that not only meets, but exceeds their expectations."

> **Ed Ploor,**
> *Senior Vice President, Data Center, Operations &*
> *Support Services*

The Ninth Core Value — Stability and Consistency

"We are well-known for being a stable and consistent organization and we want and need that reputation to continue. People like working for us for many reasons, one of which is the confidence they have that we will be around to take care of them and their families. Agents place business with us because they believe in our philosophy of evolution, not revolution when it comes to change. And policyholders come to us because they know we will be there for them when they have a claim. Stability and consistency is not only a core value, it's one big reason we have been successful."

Rod Rupp,
Senior Vice President, Claims

The Tenth Core Value — Profit

"I would advise our associates to be proud of the history of profits of Auto-Owners and to allow their profit-sharing accounts to grow for their future. Profit-sharing accounts are the result of our core values and a safe and secure method for each associate to earn additional profits."

Eileen Fhaner,
Senior Vice President and Treasurer

APPENDIX 2

Roger's Leadership Principles

1. To be a successful leader, first think of yourself as a servant.

2. Business is a team sport—keep your ego on the back burner.

3. Leaders have high expectations, then help others do and be their best by living up to those expectations.

4. People follow people they know, like, trust and respect; that means leaders must go out of their way to get to know people, and to earn their trust and respect.

5. Leadership begins with authenticity, and the best way to be more authentic is to know your strengths and weaknesses, and to work on developing your strengths.

6. Effective communication is at the heart of leadership, so effective leaders work hard to develop not only their speaking and writing skills, but also their listening skills.

7. Leadership is hard work requiring high energy; leaders first energize themselves, then share their energy with others.

8. Leaders are those who bring out the full potential of people around them; the acid test of leadership is developing new leaders.

9. Leaders are committed—they are in it for the long haul, and do not quit in the face of obstacles or setbacks; they appreciate that great accomplishments require hard work and don't happen overnight.

10. When you change your thinking, you change your beliefs. When you change your beliefs, you change your expectations. When you change your expectations, you change your attitude. When you change your attitude, you change your behavior. When you change your behavior, you change your performance. When you change your performance, you change your life.